101
THINGS
Everyone Should Know about
THEODORE ROOSEVELT

101

THINGS

Everyone Should Know about

THEODORE ROOSEVELT

ROUGH RIDER. PRESIDENT. AMERICAN ICON.

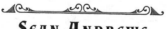

SEAN ANDREWS

ADAMS MEDIA
AVON, MASSACHUSETTS

Published by Adams Media, a division of F+W Media, Inc.
57 Littlefield Street
Avon, MA 02322 U.S.A.
www.adamsmedia.com

ISBN 10: 1-4405-7357-3
ISBN 13: 978-1-4405-7357-6
eISBN 10: 1-4405-7358-1
eISBN 13: 978-1-4405-7358-3

Printed in the United States of America.

10 9 8 7 6 5 4 3 2 1

Library of Congress Cataloging-in-Publication Data

Andrews, Sean.
    101 things everyone should know about Theodore Roosevelt / Sean Andrews.
        pages cm
    ISBN 978-1-4405-7357-6 (pb) -- ISBN 1-4405-7357-3 (pb) -- ISBN 978-1-4405-
7358-3 (eISBN) - ISBN 1-4405-7358-1 (eISBN)
    1. Roosevelt, Theodore, 1858-1919--Miscellanea. 2. Presidents--United States
--Miscellanea. I. Title. II. Title: One hundred one things everyone should know
about Theodore Roosevelt. III. Title: One hundred and one things everyone should
know about Theodore Roosevelt.
    E757.A74 2014
    973.91'1092--dc23

                                            2013034872

CONTENTS

INTRODUCTION

A Peek Into the Life of an Enigmatic Man

When Theodore Roosevelt—TR as he is called throughout this book—died in 1919, he was a medical marvel. He was deaf in one ear, blind in one eye, had a swollen ankle and a bullet in his chest . . . in short, he was not a healthy man. But that didn't stop him. He was planning a presidential campaign when he finally succumbed to his ill health. To him, afflictions like these were part of the process of living, and a person who could not overcome obstacles would never succeed. Overcoming obstacles is the central theme of TR's life.

TR was a bundle of contradictions: a literary man who loved physical pursuits; a progressive thinker who was also (in many ways) a war hawk. He came from a wealthy background, but his privilege only made him understand the importance of giving everyone a "fair deal."

This book unravels some of the mystery surrounding him and provides insights into his life so that you can understand those contradictions better—and come away with a deeper understanding of the substantial contributions he made to world history.

TR is arguably the president most responsible for making the United States the modern country that it is today. His personal philosophies shaped his actions; his personal tragedies and triumphs affected how he acted in the larger world.

TR suffered through the same vicissitudes that most people do. He enjoyed victories; he endured defeats. He made friends and enemies. He lost money in investments and saw his first wife die. Through it all, he connected with ideas, people, and the environment. He could not abide those who sat life out. In his speech, "Citizen in a Republic," given in France in 1910 (after he had left the presidency), TR spoke about the "man in the arena"—the person who is engaged in life, "who at the worst, if he fails, at least fails while daring greatly, so that his place shall never be with those cold and timid souls who neither know victory nor defeat."

TR was a motivated man who believed in deeds. Thus, some critics have looked at him as a hard person to live with. Despite such suggestions, he was neither a demon nor a deity. Theodore Roosevelt was simply a complicated person.

Yes, as TR proved, individuals can succeed regardless of societal status, physical challenges, political adversaries, and other factors that shape their lives. The challenges that TR overcame to earn his success are an inspiration to people everywhere. He was a role model, and his legacy reflects that.

Everyone can learn something from Theodore Roosevelt's life; these 101 facts are a great place to start the process.

PART 1

Early Life

FACT #1. THOUGH BORN IN A WELL-TO-DO FAMILY, ROOSEVELT HAD TO WORK HARD TO SUCCEED.

History begins anew every time a baby is born. There is no way to predict how each newborn is going to change history or whom the change will affect. Only history can tell that.

Certainly, Theodore Roosevelt's birth on October 27, 1858, led to some radical changes in world history. They began in his early years as he established the patterns in his life that shaped him into one of the world's most dynamic and enigmatic leaders, and created a legacy that endures almost a century after his death.

Although it may not seem apparent, Theodore Roosevelt was a self-made man—despite being born to a wealthy family. The shaping process began, as it does with any self-made person, when he was a child. TR recognized early in life that if he was going to be successful, he would have to earn whatever he achieved—if he lived long enough to achieve it. Even though he had been born into a privileged family, nobody was going to give him anything. That was not the Roosevelt family way.

For the Roosevelts, the road to success required action and perseverance. Inaction was not an option. TR learned that lesson in large part due to his parents' and siblings' influence.

The future U.S. president's childhood was not ordinary by any stretch of the imagination. He suffered from health problems that no family's name or wealth could prevent—he had terrible asthma and other ailments. Yet, neither he nor his family members ever used those problems as an excuse for failure or weakness. Instead, he—and his father in particular—used them as a challenge and a stepping stone to what he called a "strenuous life," a phrase TR used often as he developed physically, mentally, and emotionally.

The word "inaction" was not in Theodore Senior's lexicon. He hammered into his children the idea that laziness was a bad habit that he would not tolerate. He pushed physical activity as a remedy for laziness, especially for TR.

Theodore Senior (often called "Thee") encouraged the youngster to exercise regularly and take boxing lessons to build himself up physically. He built an in-house gymnasium for TR where he could work out. The activity paid off.

The changes in TR's physique became more noticeable as he grew older. By the time TR entered Harvard, he was a much stronger and healthier-looking person than he had been a few years earlier. His father's investment in TR had paid off.

As part of the regimen, Thee took TR on tours of the city so he could gain some knowledge of New Yorkers' living conditions and gain a feel for the plight of the people who were unfortunate enough not to be Roosevelts. He also inculcated religious lessons into the young boy.

Part of TR's assignments involved memorizing stories from the Bible. Thee believed in literally practicing what he preached, and he instilled that lesson into TR. He demanded that TR stay active in the religious arena—and in all other aspects of life.

TR never forgot his early religious training. He switched denominations at different stages of his life, but he thanked God regardless of which church he sat in. He had a lot for which to be thankful.

Teddy Trivia

A woman who lived next door to the Roosevelts told TR's friend and biographer Jacob Riis that she saw the young boy hanging from a second-story window one day. She alerted his mother, and then prepared to catch TR as he fell. She told Riis, "If the Lord had not taken care of Theodore, he would have been killed long ago."

FACT #2. ROOSEVELT'S THREE SIBLINGS PROFOUNDLY INFLUENCED HIM THROUGHOUT HIS LIFE.

Throughout his entire life, TR often turned to his family during times of trouble for help and support.

"Bamie"

Young "Teedie," a nickname he acquired early, was the second child born to Theodore Roosevelt Sr. ("Thee") and Martha Bulloch Roosevelt ("Mittie"). By the time he arrived on October 27, 1858, in the family's New York City brownstone, his older sister, Anna, was almost four years old. Anna, born on January 18, 1855, was destined to play a significant role in TR's life.

Anna and TR had two major things in common. Like him, she had to overcome serious health problems. And they were both full of seemingly boundless energy despite their ailments.

Anna, known as "Bamie," a play on the Italian word *bambina* (little girl), or "Bye," suffered from a spinal ailment. As a result, she wore confining corrective steel braces in her childhood.

The braces did not slow her down. Her disdain for them explains how she acquired her nickname. Anna came and went so fast at times that people were not sure they actually saw her. They got used to saying, "Hi, Bamie. Bye, Bamie."

Many years later, when TR was left a widower with a young baby, he needed someone to take care of her. The social conventions of the time suggested that a widower was not the proper person to raise a young daughter. Even though TR was not above breaking convention on occasion, he chose not to in this regard. Enter his sister Bamie.

Bamie was twenty-nine years old at the time. She may not have known much about child rearing, but she did know that her younger brother needed help, which she provided to his everlasting gratitude.

Elliott

The next young Roosevelt, Elliott, "Ellie" or "Nell" for short, was born sixteen months after Teedie, on February 28, 1860. That was ideal for them both from a playmate standpoint. Elliott and TR were close as children. But their lives eventually went in different directions, as Theodore developed into the best-known and most successful of the four siblings and Elliott became the pariah. No one could have predicted that in 1860, though.

Elliott and TR were highly competitive as children. Elliott served as TR's best man at his first wedding. Sadly, Elliott started drinking alcohol when he was young. Eventually, he was ostracized from the family. He survived a suicide attempt at age thirty-four, but died a few days later. That was a sad day for the Roosevelt family.

"Conie"

The fourth child, Corinne, joined the family on September 27, 1861. She, too, played an important role in TR's life—especially after his first wife died. "Conie," as she was known, formed a friendship with the Roosevelts's next-door neighbor, Edith Kermit Carow. Edith, who was born on August 6, 1861, only a few weeks before Corinne, also befriended TR. Eventually, their friendship turned into marriage.

The close family relationships among the Roosevelt children, and their love and respect for their parents, were significant factors in TR's development. The same close family relationships blossomed among TR's children after he became a father.

FACT #3. ROOSEVELT'S PARENTS WERE ON OPPOSITE SIDES WHEN IT CAME TO THE CIVIL WAR.

TR's parents were married December 22, 1853, a few years before the Civil War broke out. For the most part, family life in TR's early years was harmonious. But during the years of the Civil War, his parents had their disagreements.

Theodore Sr. (often called Thee) was a lifelong New Yorker, a noted New York City philanthropist, and a Union supporter. Like her future husband, Martha (often called Mittie) was a native of the North, at least technically. She was born in Hartford, Connecticut, on July 8, 1835, but she and her mother moved to Savannah, Georgia, when Mittie was only a few months old. (Ironically, Mittie's daughter—TR's sister—Bamie was buried in Farmington, Connecticut, just a few miles away from Hartford.)

Mittie's family members, the Bullochs, were at heart "dyed-in-the-wool" Southerners. As a result, Thee's and Martha's political allegiances became an issue when the Civil War began in April 1861.

Theodore Sr. worked for the Union, although he never served on active duty in the military. Rather, he paid a replacement to serve in his stead, which was legal at the time. That was one of the few aspects of Thee's life that he regretted.

In all fairness, Theodore Sr. may have avoided active military service in an effort to keep peace in the family, considering his wife's perspective. Instead, he served as an allotment commissioner for New York, tried to persuade soldiers to send part of their wages to their families, and traveled to Washington, D.C., to visit President Lincoln and lobby Congress for programs to support the Union troops in the field and their families.

Martha placed her loyalties with the Confederate States of America out of concern for her brothers, James Bulloch, a Confederate agent in England, and Irvine Bulloch, an officer with the Confederate Navy. Irvine was the youngest officer aboard the vaunted commerce raider CSS

Alabama, which succumbed to the U.S. Navy sloop-of-war *Kearsarge* in a historic battle off Cherbourg, France, on June 19, 1864. He was credited with firing the last gun aboard *Alabama* just before it sank.

Both brothers survived the war, as well as the rest of the immediate Roosevelt family.

Though Teddy was very young at the start of the Civil War, this family situation may have influenced him later on. For example, his eagerness to be involved in the Spanish-American War (leading the so-called "Rough Riders") may have had something to do with his father's regret over having not personally served in the Civil War.

A related story shows that TR often worked hard to understand both sides of a story—again, perhaps a habit of mind picked up during these early years. He learned early history and political science lessons from James Bulloch, who moved to England after the Civil War and became an ardent Tory (conservative). Bulloch could not abide the liberal statesman William E. Gladstone. TR sometimes defended Gladstone, much to Bulloch's dismay. TR was trying to understand both sides of an argument, which became the norm for him.

Teddy Trivia

Scarlett O'Hara, the heroine of the classic Civil War novel *Gone with the Wind*, was allegedly modeled after TR's mother Mittie.

Fact #4. Roosevelt's sister's childhood friend would become Roosevelt's second wife.

TR's sister Conie and Edith Kermit Carow, who were born only seven weeks and 109 miles apart (Edith was born in Norwich, Connecticut), were playmates, so TR, then often called "Teedie," tagged along with them. TR and Edith had a long history, which was destined to become longer after his first wife died at a very young age.

TR and Edith (called "Edie") grew up together in New York City. She was his best friend by proxy and a schoolmate of sorts. His mother invited Edie to "enroll" in the homeschool taught by the younger Roosevelts's aunt and governess.

Edie and Teedie shared some special moments in their early years. One in particular was poignant. They and Elliott Roosevelt watched President Lincoln's funeral procession pass by from an upstairs window of the Roosevelts's grandfather's house on Union Square in New York City. The Carows lived nearby on Union Square.

Thirty-six years later, another presidential assassination would play a role in Teedie's life. He would assume the presidency to replace the slain William McKinley, alongside his now-wife Edith. But that would not happen for some time after they were grown adults.

Into their early teens, the childhood friends spent a lot of time with one another. They were often together during summer events at Oyster Bay, Long Island, which was destined to become their home. They did not see one another exclusively, partly because she was three years younger than him. Edie was always on his mind, though.

Young Theodore painted the name Edith on his rowboat when he was sixteen. Their age difference came into play when he left for college. TR was seventeen years old when he started classes at Harvard. She was fourteen. The age difference was beginning to show. He was in Massachusetts; she was in New York. He was at Harvard; she was a product of Miss Comstock's Finishing School in New York City. Distance aside, they continued to share two traits in common: They were both serious students and loved books.

Teedie and Edie maintained their friendship while he was at Harvard. It changed after his father died in 1878. Exactly what happened is a mystery of history.

There is some speculation that TR proposed to Edith in the summer of 1878, but she said no. He never admitted to that and would not explain what happened to affect their relationship. He did say later, "we both of us had tempers . . . that were far from the best." At any rate, they both moved on with their lives.

Edith attended TR's October 27, 1880, marriage to Alice Hathaway Lee, but after that they drifted apart. They did not have many opportunities to socialize while he was married. They did see each other occasionally later after his wife's death, when he traveled from North Dakota to New York to visit. All in all, their get-togethers were few and far between until he returned from his North Dakota adventure in 1886—the same year she moved to London with her widowed mother.

As a sign of how close TR and Edith were as children, he gave her a pet name based on her penchant for tidiness: "Spotless Edie." Over the years, their friendship developed into a romance, although it took twenty-five years and a myriad of vicissitudes before they became husband and wife—and she became a future first lady.

FACT #5. ROOSEVELT'S POOR HEALTH IN CHILDHOOD CONTRIBUTED TO HIS INTEREST IN NATURAL HISTORY.

Thee and Mittie must have wondered after the birth of their second child if they would ever have any healthy children. Anna contended with her spinal problem. Teedie developed asthma and other ailments as a child. As a result, he often slept in a chair or sitting up in bed.

TR's breathing problems grew so severe at times during the night that his father would take him for horse rides in an attempt to open his airways. The relief was temporary, but TR did not let his persistent ailments get him down. He may have been weak physically, but he did not let that get in the way of learning.

At times, the family left New York City just to find places where TR could breathe. Even that did not always help. Corinne remembered times when he suffered tremendously, even in summer weather. But, she observed, his asthma attacks were never as bad in the summer as they were in the winter.

To compound his problems, TR was nearsighted. He joked that the only things he could study while learning about nature "were those I ran against or stumbled over." His eyesight never improved. Later in life, he lost the sight in one eye in a boxing match. In one sparring session, his partner hit him so hard below the left eye that he lost sight in it. He kept the blindness a secret and went about his business despite the impairment. He did not reveal it to anyone for a long while afterward.

In a way, TR's bad health was beneficial. It contributed to his early interest in natural history. Since he was ill and indoors so often, he had to find ways to occupy his time. Since TR was an inquisitive child, one activity was to study nature. He developed an interest in natural history that he never lost, whether it was through reading books or conducting field experiments.

Studying birds and animals and their role in nature provided a mental getaway from the rigors of whatever avenue he was pursuing at various stages of his life. He shared the knowledge he gained with the rest of the world, and provided the results of his scientific research to museums and educational institutions.

One of the first books TR read intensively was David Livingstone's *Missionary Travels and Researches in South Africa*. Livingstone's discussions of ants fascinated him. TR kept pestering everybody in the family to answer his questions about ants. Finally, Bamie had to do some research and answer his questions to give the family some peace.

Not only did TR prepare specimens for posterity; he recorded rigorous notes. One of his first "published" works was a paper titled "The Natural History of Insects," which he wrote when he was only nine years old.

TR never lost his love for animals, a love that his children inherited. In 1902, when he was in the White House, his family menagerie included "a puppy of the most orthodox puppy type," a terrier, a Chesapeake Bay dog, a macaw, a piebald rat, a flying squirrel, two kangaroo rats, and a pony. TR was as much a zookeeper as he was the president at the time.

Fact #6. As a child, Roosevelt established a "Natural History Museum"—in his bedroom!

One morning, while on an errand, TR saw a dead seal at a market. He started asking questions about where it came from and how it died. If there was one thing TR knew how to do, it was ask questions. He was a naturally curious boy. Somehow, he connected the dead seal to the adventure novels of the Irish-born writer Mayne Reid, and the seal became an obsession with TR.

TR visited the dead seal often. He measured it frequently, took notes regarding its carcass, and continued to ask questions about the animal.

One day, the seal was gone, but TR found and kept the head. It ended up in what he called the Roosevelt Natural History Museum.

TR's parents encouraged his natural history studies. A family chambermaid did not. He and two of his cousins established their natural history museum in his room, which did not get the chambermaid's seal of approval. They had to move it and other specimens they had gathered to a new location in an isolated part of the house.

From that point on, TR was hooked on natural history and planned to make it his life's work, with his father's help. Thee gave TR permission to take lessons in taxidermy when he was thirteen years old. His teacher, John G. Bell, had accompanied famed naturalist James Audubon on an expedition to the western section of the country. Even though Bell did not know much about science, he taught TR how to stuff and mount animals. That skill came in handy in TR's later years as he expanded his big-game hunting horizons.

That same summer he expanded his collection of books on mammals and birds and read them thoroughly. That led him to collecting specimens of the critters mentioned in the books, which almost led to disaster due to his poor eyesight.

TR had an old hunting gun, which he described as a "breech-loading, pin-fire double-barrel, of French manufacture." The Roosevelts were living at Dobbs Ferry, New York, at the time, a few miles up the Hudson River from New York City. Rural Dobbs Ferry was an ideal hunting ground for TR.

His gun was an excellent piece for "a clumsy and often absent-minded boy." The cartridges tended to stick at times when he tried to fire the gun, which led to misfires. As a result, he said, "[I] tattooed myself with partially unburned grains of powder more than once."

Finally, his parents stepped in to help him. That fall, he received his first pair of eyeglasses. His corrected eyesight allowed him to read more, shoot better, collect more specimens, and expand his knowledge of natural history.

Thee recognized early that TR was an avid learner. He watched with pride as his first-born son practically taught himself the basics of taxidermy and built his own wildlife museum. TR caught and killed animals, studied and stuffed them, and displayed them in his personal collection.

FACT #7. ROOSEVELT WAS HOMESCHOOLED.

TR's father Thee understood that TR's interest in natural history was laudable and beneficial, but it alone could not serve as the foundation for a well-rounded education. The young man needed to study math, history, geography, foreign languages, and other subjects, which Thee believed were best left to professional teachers. That was a dilemma for Thee.

He did not believe that TR was prepared from either a health or a physical standpoint for a regular school. The next best alternative, in his opinion, was homeschooling. Thus, Thee assumed the dual role of parent and school superintendent. That was both a benefit and a drawback for TR.

In addition to providing some of the lessons himself, Thee employed several tutors, including TR's maternal aunt, Annie Bulloch, and a French governess.

For a few months, the youngster attended a school run by Professor John McMullen, Thee's former tutor. But TR acquired his early education mostly through homeschooling—which put him automatically at or near the head of his class.

Mittie and Annie related stories from their own childhoods to entertain and educate the Roosevelt children. They recounted their lives on the Georgia plantations; related tales of hunting fox, deer, wildcats, and other animals; and spun stories of their long-tailed driving horses, Boone and Crockett. When TR grew older, he founded a hunting club named after those two horses.

Thee could provide the subject background for a classical education and moral training. But he could only go so far in providing the social skills that complemented the coursework. Granted, TR had friends and a family network who helped him develop socially. But most children of his age attended private schools where they received well-rounded educations, developed complementary social skills, and participated in competitive physical activities.

In those respects, TR's homeschooling was a detriment in his early years. Even he recognized, albeit much later, that he was not the most mature young man in New York City for the first few years of his life.

Thee did not neglect his oldest son's moral and religious training. Since he was a firm believer in religion and morality, he made sure to include liberal doses of both in his children's training.

By the time TR was ready to leave his New York home and enter Harvard, he had matured mentally, spiritually, morally, and physically—although he was still not as robust as he needed to be to survive on his own. He continued his development process at school.

FACT #8. BEFORE ATTENDING HARVARD, ROOSEVELT HAD TO MAKE UP FOR LOST TIME WITH THE HELP OF A DEMANDING TUTOR.

TR's homeschooling provided some benefits that were above average even among his peers. Whereas some students had to study geography through books, TR got to study it up close and personal. The family traveled through Europe twice, in 1869 and 1870, and through the Middle East in 1872–1873. That beat reading books as far as TR and his siblings were concerned.

Despite this advantage, in his early teens TR was not prepared to enter Harvard (and of course it was expected he would go to college). He needed a considerable amount of preparatory schooling before he could begin his studies there. TR possessed a great deal of knowledge, much of which he had learned from practical experience. That alone was not going to get him into Harvard. He realized that. He explained, "I could not go to school because I knew so much less than most boys of my age in some subjects and so much more in others."

TR himself recognized the value of a college education, especially if he wanted to accomplish everything he had in mind. For him, that meant an opportunity to pursue his studies in natural history. (Ironically, his stay at Harvard sidetracked him from achieving that dream.)

He was well versed in science, history, geography, German, and French. He needed to strengthen other liberal arts subjects. So he worked with a tutor his father hired to start his preparation for an Ivy League education.

After the family returned from an overseas tour in the winter of 1872–1873, Thee employed Arthur Cutler, a recent Harvard graduate, to work exclusively with TR. Cutler developed a program for his student, designed to strengthen the academic areas in which he was most lacking, such as mathematics and classical languages, specifically Latin and Greek.

Teddy Trivia

Cutler may have been TR's superior in academic skills, but not in physical strength. In 1879, on a hiking trip in Maine, they climbed Mt. Katahdin with a guide, Bill Sewall. Normally, the climb up the 5,268-foot mountain took days. Even though TR was carrying a 45-pound pack, he made it to the top. Cutler did not.

The program Cutler designed was meant to take three years to complete. TR was equal to the challenge. He worked six to eight hours a day and finished the curriculum in two years. By that time he had polished his mathematics, Greek, and Latin skills to the point where he did well enough on the Harvard entrance exams to gain admittance.

A look back at his entrance exams shows that even then TR demonstrated a predilection for choosing subjects that interested him. He focused on subjects like mathematics and placed very little emphasis on the classics. His strategy worked. He was one of the few freshmen in his class at Harvard to take advanced mathematics courses.

Cutler did wonders preparing TR for a big step in his life.

FACT #9. ROOSEVELT WAS RAISED IN THE ERA OF "MUSCULAR CHRISTIANITY."

Although Thee encouraged his son's interest in science, he taught him the values of Muscular Christianity (faith through piety and physical fitness) by taking him on his missionary rounds. He insisted that TR memorize Bible stories and taught him the principles of patriotism and manly valor. He chastised laziness, demanding constant action.

The term "Muscular Christianity" appears occasionally throughout literature, often with no explanation. A deranged preacher in Robert B. Parker's Western novel, *Brimstone*, set in the 1880s, told a marshal advising him of trouble, "An armed and muscular Christianity cannot be defeated." The author did not explain that it was an actual movement—one that affected TR's childhood and young adulthood.

When TR arrived at Harvard, he found it difficult to break his ties with Thee, which complicated his life on campus at first.

Thee espoused some eccentric ideas that redounded badly on his family at times. One of them was his belief in Muscular Christianity as it related to masculinity—and Harvard.

The Roosevelts were devout Christians. TR never lost his belief in God or Christianity, and his religious fervor pushed away some of his classmates when he arrived on campus. He may have agreed with Thee when it came to religious beliefs, but father and son differed when it came to sexism.

Thee believed that men were the stronger and more moralistic gender.

TR always saw women and children as strong people who could benefit from the support of males. Thee carried his belief about male superiority over into the religious realm. His connection between the two worlds led to problems for TR.

In Thee's mind, men were becoming emasculated by the mid-nineteenth century—at least in New York City. He theorized that one way to restore their disappearing zest for life and morality was to build up their bodies, which he thought would be good for TR. Thus, he was a strong proponent of Muscular Christianity. After all, Muscular Christianity advocates averred, Jesus Christ was morally pure and physically fit. His advocates should follow suit. That philosophy fit well into Thee's "private trainer" program for TR.

Thee began pushing TR almost from birth to strengthen his body through constant physical activity. He thought that what was good for TR was good for the rest of his children, the young people of New York City, and beyond. Thee used his philanthropic bent to promote Muscular Christianity and build a better, more masculine world.

Some of TR's fellow students at Harvard believed that he pushed the Muscular Christianity concept too far. They viewed his focus on the "strenuous life" as a bit bizarre, even though some of them marveled at his physical prowess. Stories of his athletic endeavors, energy, and enthusiasm for just about everything abounded.

Part 2

The College Years

FACT #10. ROOSEVELT HAD DIFFICULTY ADJUSTING TO HARVARD AND WAS CALLED A "LOUD-MOUTHED ATTENTION-GRABBER."

The transition from home to Harvard was difficult for TR. He was used to the informal homeschool environment at the family home and to his limited circle of friends. TR found that Harvard was an unforgiving place for him at first. He adapted, but slowly.

TR may have been ready for Harvard—academically speaking, anyway—but there was some question as to whether Harvard was ready for him. He arrived at the college with an air of smugness and condescension that his fellow students found difficult to tolerate.

Once he learned that there was more to college than studying, he began to develop his mind and body, and found a wider circle of friends. Eventually, he graduated with high honors, a healthy attitude, a widely expanded store of knowledge—and a soon-to-be wife.

Another criticism of TR at Harvard centered on his penchant for grabbing attention. He occasionally broke the unwritten rules of decorum that suggested students should be quiet when passing each other in the halls or on the grounds. And he was always running when everyone else was walking.

Perhaps some of his classmates might have thought he was trying to gain attention. But, that was simply the way TR did everything: full speed ahead, which (eventually) helped him earn respect from his classmates.

TR was not a big man when he entered college. He was about five feet nine inches tall and weighed 135 pounds. To him, size did not matter. What he lacked in size he made up for in stamina and courage. TR used those assets to gain the respect of his classmates.

Somehow, TR completed his studies in the allotted four years at Harvard and graduated Phi Beta Kappa, an honor which recognizes and encourages scholarship, friendship, and cultural interests at the undergraduate level. That was not easy, considering that he had failed a couple of courses along the way and did not write an honors thesis.

Not surprisingly, TR's best grades were in natural history, where he averaged in the high eighties and nineties. He failed two courses, Greek and French. There is no telling what he could have done if he had applied himself.

There is some discrepancy about TR's overall average at Harvard. Estimates range from 80.5 to 87. Regardless, he graduated magna cum laude (with great honor) and finished in the top tenth of his 174-member class, although he was not sure if it was the tenth of the whole number who entered or of those who graduated. Either way, TR had a college degree—and an achievement to be proud of.

Teddy Trivia

TR developed a few friendships at Harvard. The most cherished friend, however, was a young lady named Alice Hathaway Lee, whom he met on October 18, 1878. She changed his life forever. Soon, she became his primary interest. He found himself chasing two goals at the same time: his degree and a wife.

FACT #11. ROOSEVELT DEVELOPED A PASSION FOR BOXING AT HARVARD.

TR developed a passion for boxing while at Harvard. He engaged in bouts with classmates both in the ring and outside. Frederic Almy, the secretary of TR's class of 1880, related an event that occurred during the controversial 1876 presidential campaign between Republican Rutherford B. Hayes and Democrat Samuel J. Tilden. The polling was hotly debated. Tilden won the popular vote and had a lead in the electoral count, 184 to 165, with twenty disputed votes uncounted. After a protracted legal and political battle, the disputed votes were awarded to Hayes. Incidentally, Hayes was the first president to graduate from law school (Harvard Law School, 1845).

As Almy recalled, there was a torchlight parade in progress when a person on the sidewalk near TR made a derogatory comment. TR reacted violently and rashly.

Almy said that he "reached out and laid the mucker flat." That was uncharacteristic of TR for two reasons: He was not prone to solve arguments through physical means, and he had not developed a great fondness for politics at that point—although it is true that he did become interested in politics during his Harvard years.

TR did not play on any intercollegiate teams, but one of his favorite activities ended up being boxing. He would take on all comers in sparring matches or tournaments. TR did not win any championships, but he won some of his classmates over to his side.

In March 1879, TR won a match in a lightweight boxing tournament at Harvard. As it ended, the referee called, "Time!" Just as TR dropped his hands, his opponent punched him hard in the face. The crowd protested and screamed, "Foul!" TR allegedly told them to quiet down. "He did not hear," TR explained. That indicated his sense of fair play.

Another classmate, Richard Welling, related endurance contests they took part in. Welling, like TR, was a physical training devotee. One extremely cold afternoon the two young men went skating on a local pond. Neither one was particularly adept at skating. Under ordinary circumstances they would have hung up their skates, gone inside, and warmed up. But neither would admit that they were close to suffering frostbite.

TR kept asking Welling, "Isn't this perfectly bully?" Welling did not think so, but he would not say anything to destroy TR's feigned enthusiasm. He just agreed. The test of wills continued. Finally, well into their third hour of skating—at least as Welling reported—TR suggested they stop. It was one of the rare times that TR found himself on thin ice and gave up—if he did.

Philip M. Boffey, who wrote an article about TR's life at Harvard, cautioned, "So many legends have grown up around Theodore Roosevelt that it is hard to sift fact from fiction. A host of friends, classmates, and distant admirers have felt obliged to produce anecdotes about this 'locomotive in human pants,' thus swelling the collection of stories over the years."

Teddy Trivia

TR admitted that he was not good at the sport of boxing. But he entered one tournament at the school in which he did pretty well. He reached the semifinals or finals (he could not remember which). TR considered that a major achievement, even though he admitted that it was one of his rare athletic accomplishments.

FACT #12. *THE NAVAL WAR OF 1812* WAS ROOSEVELT'S FIRST PUBLISHED BOOK, WRITTEN WHEN HE SHOULD HAVE BEEN ATTENDING CLASSES.

One of TR's major accomplishments during his time at Harvard was his authorship of *The Naval War of 1812*, although TR belittled it afterward. He completed it years later when he was in law school at Columbia. While at Columbia, TR became disillusioned with what he was learning and transferred his energy from studying law to completing the book and working on behalf of the consumers he believed were getting a raw deal instead of a fair deal.

The Naval War of 1812 was published in 1882, the year he should have received his JD degree. He decided the law degree could wait. TR dropped out of law school to work for justice as it related to his vision of the law.

He noted in his self-deprecating fashion, "Those chapters were so dry that they would make a dictionary seem light reading by comparison." Readers did not agree with his assessment after the book was published.

TR commented that the chapters he wrote represented "purpose and serious interest on my part, not the perfunctory effort to do well enough to get a certain mark." He revealed, "Corrections of them by a skilled older man would have impressed me and have commanded my respectful attention."

Certainly, when TR was writing *The Naval War of 1812*, he had no way of knowing that he would someday become assistant secretary of the navy and open himself up to some of the same criticisms he heaped on American commanders and political leaders during the war. In Chapter VIII of *The Naval War of 1812*, he discussed their extreme caution, sometimes "verging on timidity." And, he claimed that the land segment of the war was not worth studying.

In *The Naval War of 1812*, TR wrote:

> *But a short examination showed that these operations were hardly worth serious study. They teach nothing new; it is the old, old lesson, that a miserly economy in preparation may in the end involve a lavish outlay of men and money, which, after all, comes too late to more than partially offset the evils produced by the original short-sighted parsimony.*

TR also observed, "At present people are beginning to realize that it is folly for the great English-speaking Republic to rely for defence [sic] upon a navy composed partly of antiquated hulks, and partly of new vessels rather more worthless than the old." Those words would help him later on in life when building a strong navy became his responsibility.

Perhaps it was the arrogance of his youth and inexperience in political and military matters at the time that encouraged him to include these observations, but he stored the lessons he learned and applied them in later years. That was one of his strong points: He learned from everything he did and used his knowledge for positive purposes later. And, more often than not, what he learned became the subject of subsequent books and articles.

FACT #13. ROOSEVELT SUFFERED A MAJOR TRAGEDY DURING HIS YEARS AT HARVARD WHEN HIS FATHER DIED.

Halfway through TR's stay at Harvard, a major tragedy occurred. On February 9, 1878, TR's father died of stomach cancer. That was a bitter blow for the young man, who had enjoyed a close relationship with Theodore Sr. for almost twenty years. TR made no bones about his admiration for his father. He said, "I never knew anyone who got greater joy out of living than did my father, or anyone who more whole-heartedly performed every duty; and no one whom I have ever met approached his combination of enjoyment of life and performance of duty."

Thee had opened TR's eyes to the fact that not everybody lived as well as the Roosevelts did. Thee made sure that his family visited people in all strata of society. On Thanksgiving or Christmas Day he sometimes took TR and his siblings to dinner at places like the Newsboys' Lodging House or Miss Slattery's Night School for Little Italians, both of which he had a hand in establishing.

The Newsboys' Lodging House was one of Thee's pet projects. He was also active in getting orphaned and homeless children off the streets and out of the city. He arranged as often as possible to get them placed on farms in the West. Thee helped form the Children's Aid Society in New York City, which built institutions for homeless children and originated "orphan trains" to transport them to the western part of the United States. For a while, Thee visited the Newsboys' Lodging House every Sunday night and sponsored dinners there. TR picked up temporarily where his father left off after he graduated from college in 1880.

TR always recalled fondly the lessons he learned from his father. Thee taught him and his siblings about their duties to society. His father was religious, brave, gentle, tender, unselfish, and, most of all, loving. He instilled those same virtues in his children.

And Thee made it clear there were certain things he would not tolerate in them. Selfishness, cruelty, idleness, cowardice, and lack of truthfulness topped the list. Thee relied on discipline and love to drive those virtues and vices into his children's minds.

Above all, Thee made his children feel protected. TR always felt safe with Thee, but he knew that the protection only went so far. Thee expected the children to fight their own battles when necessary. He knew he would not be around forever to help them. Self-dependence was one of the biggest gifts he gave his children. It was one that TR learned well.

Thee was not averse to giving his children little gifts every now and then. That practice reinforced the notion of giving, even if the little things he gave had no extrinsic value but served merely as reminders of a father's love for his children. TR passed the same types of gifts to his children later on.

Teddy Trivia

TR invented his own reward system with his children. He remembered one in particular. Whichever child brought him his bootjack, a small tool that helped people pull their boots off, after he returned from a horse ride got to walk around the room in TR's boots. That was a significant reward; it took someone special to fill his shoes.

FACT #14. ROOSEVELT ALWAYS CLAIMED HE NEVER LEARNED MUCH AT HARVARD.

The death of his father while TR was at Harvard affected TR deeply, but he continued his studies. Despite the fact he claimed that he did not learn much of value at Harvard, he did well academically there.

TR did occasionally enter classrooms. They were not his favorite places on campus, though. He admitted that he did not have much interest in the academic side of the school, which was the primary reason he enrolled at Harvard.

TR's avowed purpose in attending Harvard was to study natural history. Once he arrived on campus, he discovered that the curriculum was not geared toward the sciences. It was, after all, a liberal arts college. He compensated through physical activities and a perfunctory interest in the courses that were available.

One of his favorite professors was A.S. Hill, who taught English. TR developed a fondness for Elizabethan poetry, much to the amusement of some of his classmates.

History was also a favorite subject of his. It stimulated his interest in politics, as one of the topics on which he concentrated was the Federalist Papers. Later in his political career, he often used them as a starting point for solving problems.

Although TR was an avid reader, textbooks were not his favorite source of knowledge. He said he learned more from his favorite magazine, *Our Young Folks*, than he did from any textbook he ever read. TR claimed that everything in the magazine "instilled the individual virtues, and the necessity of character as the chief factor in any man's success—a teaching in which I now believe as sincerely as ever." The magazine taught him the "right stuff," which shaped his life.

TR believed "All the laws that the wit of man can devise will never make a man a worthy citizen unless he has within himself the right stuff, unless he has self-reliance, energy, courage, the power of insisting on his own rights and the sympathy that makes him regardful of the rights of others."

TR did not discount completely the value of the textbooks he used at Harvard. He acknowledged that he learned something from them, but they were merely supplementary to the other books he had read at home prior to entering college. It was from all those books combined that he learned the individual morality that he applied in every phase of his life.

TR believed firmly in a college education. He had a quaint way of saying that it opened up a door or two for anybody, whether for good or for bad. TR advised, "A man who has never gone to school may steal from a freight car, but if he has a university education, he may steal from the whole railroad."

Teddy Trivia

"All this individual morality I was taught by the books I read at home and the books I studied at Harvard. But there was almost no teaching of the need for collective action, and of the fact that in addition to, not as a substitute for, individual responsibility, there is a collective responsibility." – Theodore Roosevelt

FACT #15. ROOSEVELT HAD A PHOTOGRAPHIC MEMORY AND THE ABILITY TO SPEED-READ.

TR may not have had a high opinion of textbooks or the lessons that complemented them, but he read them (he also wrote them—no matter what his job at the time, TR usually had a book manuscript he was working on). Books contained new thoughts and ideas that intrigued him and that he couldn't learn any other way. That explained why he read as many books as he did throughout his life and what facilitated the process.

He possessed two valuable assets to help him satisfy his reading habit: a photographic memory and the ability to speed-read.

It was amazing to some people how much and how fast TR could read and retain. He could read a page while other people were reading a sentence or repeat stories from a newspaper he had just put down as if he were still reading it.

TR could easily read two or three books a day. When TR traveled, he always took along a sufficient number of books to educate and amuse himself with. He also used reading as an escape—and he read some esoteric material at times.

A classic example of his retreat into books occurred in the hours leading up to TR's nomination as vice president at the 1900 Republican Convention. He was sitting quietly in another room, impervious to all the excitement. He was relaxing by reading Thucydides. His companion at the time, Albert Shaw, said he "was not reading [Thucydides'] book as much as he was living it."

TR's ability to read quickly and absorb information made him one of the most intellectually talented presidents in U.S. history. Some of his predecessors may have been more versed in the classics, but TR was better equipped to digest facts on issues that mattered to statesmen, such as military history and affairs, economics, and business statistics. His experience at Harvard helped him develop his reading, concentration, and retention skills.

In addition to these skills, TR was noted for having an unshakeable attention span. Charles William Eliot, the president of Harvard when TR was in attendance, recalled his remarkable power of concentration. Although TR confessed that he rarely saw Eliot, the president knew about him.

TR lamented the lack of science courses at Harvard. Ironically, Eliot is remembered for expanding the range of courses during his tenure and offering undergraduates unlimited choices in selecting from the list. He wanted them to discover their "natural bents" and pursue them into specialized studies.

Eliot stated that "the intellectual power which most attracted the attention of his [TR's] companions and teachers was an extraordinary capacity for concentrating every faculty on the work at hand, whether it were reading, writing, listening, or boxing."

He added that TR "would read by himself in a room half-filled with noisy students without having his attention distracted even for an instant; indeed, he would make no answer to questions addressed directly to him, and did not seem to hear them." That was a talent that TR never lost.

FACT #16. ONE OF ROOSEVELT'S FAVORITE PASTIMES AT HARVARD WAS JOINING CLUBS.

TR became a "joiner" at Harvard. When he wasn't boxing, engaging in endurance contests, or studying, he was participating in a club activity of some sort. He was connected with *The Advocate*, Harvard's undergraduate journal of fiction, poetry, art, and criticism, and the O. K. Society, a group of the publication's editors, which included him.

At various times he was a member and vice president of the Natural History Society, the Art Club, the Finance Club, the Glee Club, the Harvard Rifle Corps, and the Harvard Athletic Association.

His position as editor reflected TR's enthusiasm and penchant for challenging authorities. In 1916, on the fiftieth anniversary of the publication's founding, Albert Bushnell Hart, then head of the government department at Harvard and a classmate of TR's, talked about the newspaper in 1880. He noted that those were turbulent days.

TR was by far the most honored member of the Harvard Class of 1880 when it came to advanced degrees, honorary degrees, and society memberships. Only one classmate came close: Albert Bushnell Hart. His resume included a PhD in history, an LLD, honorary degrees from Tufts (1905) and Western Reserve (1907), and a LittD. He became a professor of history and a member of the Massachusetts Historical Society.

Hart hastened to add that it was not because TR was editor. Rather, he said, "The entire board was a fighting organization, with definite ideas of needed reforms and a positive manner in urging them."

TR also joined the Hasty Pudding Club, the oldest collegiate social club in the United States; the "Dickey," the nickname for the Institute of 1770, the oldest club at Harvard; and the prestigious Porcellian Club (The "Pork"). The Porcellian, a men-only group, was the last club a student could join prior to graduation. For that reason, it was called a "final club."

Membership in such clubs, particularly the "Dickey," drew charges of snobbery from some of TR's classmates. "Dickey" members often ate off campus in small groups, away from school activities. TR did the same thing. He was not particularly concerned at that point about what other students thought of him or his eating habits. He was simply doing the right things to establish his place in the Harvard caste system and his college legacy.

Some of the clubs to which he belonged were offshoots of his interests, e.g., the Natural History Society, the Harvard Rifle Corps, and the Harvard Athletic Association. He was in the Glee Club as an associate member, which indicated that it was not one of his primary interests. He did prioritize his club activities.

The clues to the clubs in which TR was mostly interested lay in the paraphernalia in his room. Among the items he had there were a rifle, a hunting kit, and trophies from his hunting expeditions. He also had live turtles and insects in the room.

Even though TR belonged to many clubs, he was never overextended. He rarely attended meetings of some of them. TR needed some time to study. He was an unorthodox student, but he still did well when it came to grades—sometimes.

FACT #17. ROOSEVELT MET HIS FUTURE WIFE (ALICE HATHAWAY LEE) DURING HIS TIME AT HARVARD.

Near the beginning of his junior year at Harvard, TR visited the home of his classmate Richard Saltonstall in Chestnut Hill, Massachusetts. He always remembered the exact date: October 18, 1878. Saltonstall's cousin and next-door neighbor, Alice Hathaway Lee, was there. Later,

TR wrote, "As long as I live, I shall never forget how sweetly she looked, and how prettily she greeted me." This love was a new experience for him.

Their meeting would change his life dramatically. It affected everything he did from then on—at least for the next four years.

What caught TR's eye was a statuesque young lady about five feet seven inches tall, an inch or so shorter than him, with light brown hair and blue eyes. She had barely turned seventeen when they first met. Within a month of meeting Alice, TR decided he was going to marry her.

Alice possessed both inner and outer beauty and intelligence to match. Her nickname, "Sunshine," captured her demeanor perfectly as far as TR was concerned. She certainly brought a lot of sunshine into his life.

Like TR, Alice came from a large family. She was the second of six children. The first five were girls. Her only brother, George Jr., was not born until 1871. (He, too, graduated from Harvard, with the class of 1894.) TR and Alice Lee had anything but a whirlwind courtship. She dragged it out much longer than TR preferred.

Although TR had fallen in love immediately, Alice took her time deciding how she felt about him. It may have been because of her youth. He was almost three years older than Alice. Or it might have been because of his somewhat odd appearance at the time. He was thin, pale, sported long hair and a mustache, and wore eyeglasses.

The real reason she demurred is anyone's guess. But, while she "shined," he pined.

TR filled pages of his diary with accounts of his love, their activities, and the lengths to which he would go to see her. He wrote in his diary on February 3, 1880, "Snowing heavily, but I drove over in my sleigh to Chestnut Hill, the horse plunging to his belly in great drifts, and the wind cutting my face like a knife."

TR just could not believe his luck. He wrote in his diary a few months after he met her, "It seems hardly possible that I can kiss her and hold her in my arms; she is so pure and so innocent, and is very, very pretty. I have never done anything to deserve such great fortune." He decided to push his luck and her, too. TR did everything he could to get her to marry him.

He even turned the staid old Porcellian Club on its ears when he ushered Alice in for lunch. That was reportedly the first time any member had brought a woman into the club. It was unorthodox, but TR specialized in doing things that had never been done. Red tape, bureaucracy, tradition, anti-female rules . . . nothing stood in the way of love—or much of anything else—as far as TR was concerned. When he wanted something, he went after it. He kept up the pursuit; she continued to put him off.

FACT #18. ALICE WAS THE FIRST PERSON TO CALL ROOSEVELT "TEDDY."

As soon as TR met Alice, his interest in his studies and campus activities dwindled. There were two pieces of solid evidence that he was in love: He let Alice call him "Teddy" and he interrupted his naturalist expeditions.

Most of TR's family members called him "Teedie" when he was a child. The nickname did not follow him to Harvard. Alice started calling him "Teddy." He confessed later that he was never fond of that nickname, but she could have gotten away with calling him a lot worse because he was so much in love with her.

Alice was also responsible to some degree for his diminished interest in ornithology. TR wrote a letter in 1879 to his close friend and Harvard classmate Henry Davis Minot to tell him about his new romance and that he had not done any collecting of specimens to think of that year. That was a startling admission from TR, who had been addicted to natural history since his very young days. And he did things that were out of the ordinary even for him.

TR attended club meetings rarely after he met Alice. Occasionally, he took her with him. At one Hasty Pudding gathering he pointed Alice out to a group of people and vowed that he was going to marry her, even though, he said, "She won't have me."

In June 1879, TR proposed to Alice. She procrastinated for months. Finally, at the beginning of 1880, she agreed to marry him. He spent February 13, 1880, with the Lee family at their home in Chestnut Hill. The next day the couple announced their engagement.

A July 4, 1880, entry in TR's diary showed that his love was growing day by day. He wrote, "Not one thing is ever hidden between us. No matter how long I live I know my love for her will only grow deeper and tenderer day by day; and she always will be mistress over all that I have."

TR returned to Cambridge to announce their engagement. One of the first people TR told was Henry Minot.

He sent a letter to his old friend and asked him to keep the engagement secret—which TR could not do himself. He said, "I write to you to announce my engagement to Miss Alice Lee; but do not speak of it till Monday. I have been in love with her for nearly two years now, and have made everything subordinate to winning her; so you can perhaps understand a change in my ideas as regards science, etc." He could not wait for the wedding.

They married on October 27, 1880—his twenty-second birthday.

Among the guests was TR's childhood friend Edith Carow, who would also attend his second wedding a few years later—as his second wife.

TR's wedding to Alice was the greatest birthday present he could have received, but the joy was short-lived. The happy couple moved to New York City to take up residence as he started his career.

FACT #19. AFTER HARVARD, ROOSEVELT MADE A BRIEF STOP AT COLUMBIA LAW SCHOOL.

When TR graduated from Harvard, he faced a dilemma common to his peers: what to do with the rest of his life. Even though Thee had left him a comfortable inheritance, TR did not want to live off it. He returned to New York City to study law.

Perhaps the most glossed over period of TR's life is his brief stop at Columbia Law School. He accomplished some wonderful things in the short time he was there, but they were not connected to his presence in any classrooms. Yet the lessons he learned at Columbia contributed to his success as he became more accomplished later in life.

TR's choice of law school was based more on a need to find a profession than on a passion. He admitted freely that he did not have to go to law school, or any other type of school, after completing his studies at Harvard.

Money was not an issue for TR. As he put it, "I had enough to get bread. What I had to do, if I wanted butter and jam, was to provide the butter and jam, but to count their cost as compared with other things. In other words, I made up my mind that, while I must earn money, I could afford to make earning money the secondary instead of the primary object of my career."

The money Thee had left TR provided him with a cushion to fall back on. He could have idled away his time in leisurely pursuits if that had been his preference. But TR was a Roosevelt. That was not what Roosevelts did.

The family tradition was to meet social responsibilities. TR honored that charge. But his decision to pursue a profession was not easy. He looked at the future, as well as the present, when deciding what to do. That helped steer him toward Columbia Law School, which turned out to be a secondary pursuit.

A career in law would satisfy his desire to work in a field that allowed him to treat the work as more important than the money he earned performing it. So he entered Columbia Law School in 1880, filled with enthusiasm and idealism. Both faded quickly.

Even though TR never completed his law studies, he had learned some valuable studies in the pursuit of his degree. He proved that not all law has to be learned from textbooks—especially as it pertains to the administration of social justice.

While at law school, TR began attending political meetings. The more TR became embroiled in the machinations of politics, the more law school became a distant memory. Politics pushed the practice of law to the back of TR's career path.

FACT #20. ROOSEVELT LEFT LAW SCHOOL WITHOUT GRADUATING BECAUSE THE TEACHINGS OF LAW SCHOOL WENT AGAINST HIS PERSONAL PHILOSOPHY OF A "FAIR DEAL."

When he enrolled in law school, for one of the few times in his life, TR started something he did not finish. But what seemed to be a bad choice at first soon led to a promising career in politics.

Once TR began his studies at Columbia, he realized his heart was not in the program. The most significant thing he learned there was that the law was too often on the wrong side of the business and political spectrums, at least as far as his youthful idealism perceived it. That was an eye-opener for TR, and the realization changed his life goals—and ultimately many other people's lives.

TR noted, "When I left Harvard, I took up the study of law. If I had been sufficiently fortunate to come under Professor [James Bradley] Thayer, of the Harvard Law School, it may well be that I would have realized that the lawyer can do a great work for justice and against legalism." He labeled Thayer "the greatest Professor of Law Harvard ever had." However, TR did not have the opportunity to study under Professor Thayer and so did not at the time see how a law school education could help him achieve his ends.

The young, idealistic TR believed that the *caveat emptor* side of both the law and business seemed repellent. It did not, in his view, make for social fair dealing. The words "fair deal" had been—and continued to be—important to TR throughout his life.

In his view, the law ruling transactions between sellers and consumers should have struck a balance between the two: Both should have profited mutually. But what he heard from professors and what he read in law books weighted the balance in favor of the sellers, which to him was an injustice. That realization dampened his interest in becoming a lawyer.

TR did not want to engage in a curriculum or a profession that ran contrary to his personal beliefs.

TR left Columbia in 1881. He did not walk away without a plan or because he had learned enough about the law in one year to make him an expert. TR had reached a point at which he wanted to engage in politics.

Entering politics was not a new idea for TR. He had begun developing an interest in politics while he was at Harvard. By 1881, TR felt that the time was right to transfer his desire into action. Some of the things he learned while at Columbia, which had nothing to do with the study of law, pushed him in that direction.

In TR's opinion, the job of "doing good" for others placed a lot of pressure on politicians who, at some point, would be forced to step aside at least temporarily and pursue another line of work. That belief was one of the reasons he entered Columbia in the first place.

TR bravely entered politics without another occupation to fall back on.

FACT #21. COLUMBIA LAW SCHOOL EVENTUALLY GRANTED ROOSEVELT A LAW DEGREE—IN 2008.

TR may not have graduated from Columbia Law School with his class, but the *New York Times* reported he "studied law in the office of his uncle in this city, and was admitted to the bar." It did not always require completion of formal studies to attain a goal.

Eventually, TR received his law degree—several, in fact. Harvard granted him an honorary LLD in 1902. The University of California, Berkeley, followed suit a year later. He did not waste the trip to California.

The honorary degrees TR received from Harvard and Berkeley were among a handful he gathered over the years. He was not a great fan of honorary degrees. Sometimes he could not turn them down without offending his friends, which TR was always loath to do.

Columbia finally got around to presenting TR with a law degree—almost a century after his death. At a September 25, 2008, reception ceremony in New York City, the school presented an LLD to its former student. It also granted one to Franklin Delano Roosevelt on the same day.

There is no telling how TR would have felt about receiving a law degree. He was never fond of receiving honors that he had not earned. He felt that a young man should set his sights on something he truly wanted and believed in, and that using law school as a stop-gap measure was a wasted opportunity. His ambivalence was apparent when his son Theodore Jr. was deliberating between entering the Army or Naval Academy and pursuing a civilian profession.

TR wrote to his son in a January 21, 1904, letter:

The result would be that at twenty-five you would leave the Army or Navy without having gone through any law school or any special technical school of any kind, and would start your life work three or four years later than your schoolfellows of to-day, who go to work immediately after leaving college. Of course, under such circumstances, you might study law, for instance, during the four years after graduation; but my own feeling is that a man does good work chiefly when he is in something which he intends to make his permanent work, and in which he is deeply interested.

Those words came straight from TR's heart—and from his own experience of using law school as a time-filler. He might not have agreed with the administrators at Columbia when they got around to granting him a law degree.

Columbia Law School Dean David M. Schizer had kind words to say about the Roosevelts in 2008. "We are pleased to commemorate the Presidents Roosevelts, two of the most remarkable and distinguished lawyers ever to train at Columbia Law School, and celebrate their connection to our storied history," he said. The honor came too late for TR to appreciate.

Teddy Trivia

TR and his distant cousin Franklin Delano Roosevelt had one thing in common: Both left Columbia Law School before they completed their degrees. The school conferred JD degrees on both Roosevelts posthumously. They became official members of the classes of 1882 and 1907, respectively.

PART 3

Entering Politics

FACT #22. ROOSEVELT MAY HAVE BEEN THE FIRST RINO (REPUBLICAN IN NAME ONLY).

TR learned that the only political party open to him was the Republicans, due to two factors: He was considered an aristocrat and the Democrats were too rough for a young man of his upbringing. Consequently, he started attending meetings of the Twenty-First District Republican Association. He recalled, "At that day, a young man of my bringing up and convictions could only join the Republican party, and join it accordingly I did." He may have been labeled a Republican, but he manifested Democratic tendencies throughout his lifetime.

His friends looked at his dabbling in politics with disdain. Powerful businessmen and lawyers with whom he was acquainted scoffed at him because they considered politics beneath their dignity. Their role was to let rougher men do the grunt work while they used their influence to grease the wheels of government in order to get things done.

TR never forgot their cavalier attitude toward politicians and the general public in general, for whom he worked so diligently. TR may not have known much about the ins and outs of politics in 1881, but he did know how to ingratiate himself with the right people. He sensed that if he became close to the leaders at the lower levels of the party, they would think of him when the right opportunity came along. His strategy worked.

The lessons TR learned in his first foray into politics served him well throughout his government career and justified his decision to leave law school.

One of the first things he learned was that a politician could buck a machine and still come out ahead. He proved that when he became embroiled in an internal power struggle between his good friend and party stalwart Joe Murray and the Republican boss at the time, Jake Hess.

Murray was working his way up through the party structure at the time, and he "adopted" TR as his protégé. Hess also had a soft spot for TR. At the time, one of the few things Hess and Murray had in common was their recognition that the young Roosevelt was an up-and-coming star in the Republican Party. TR got caught in the power struggle between Hess and Murray, and played the game to perfection.

The issue that won Hess and Murray over to TR's side was trivial. It concerned a nonpartisan approach to street cleaning. TR backed the method in defiance of the "machine." He and the faction that was against the street cleaning practice, led by Hess and Murray, forced a vote on the idea. They all knew that TR did not have a chance of winning the vote.

As expected, his side drew about six votes of the 300 to 400 cast. TR recalled that he accepted the results in a good-humored fashion. But they did not change his attitude about bucking the machine to fight for something in which he believed. Murray in particular took note of that.

FACT #23. ROOSEVELT WAS SURPRISED TO BE NOMINATED AS NEW YORK ASSEMBLYMAN IN 1881.

As the 1881 elections approached, the Republicans were looking for a candidate for assemblyman from their district. (The Assembly was the lower house of the New York State Legislature.)

New York City Republican leaders saw something special in TR when he entered politics after graduating from Harvard, and so Joe Murray, TR's good friend, spotted an opportunity for TR to run for office. Jake Hess, the Republican boss, did not agree with Murray's proposal to nominate TR, who he believed was too young and inexperienced. (Both Hess and Murray were district leaders at the time.) Murray prevailed. The end result gave TR the opportunity to run for office as an assemblyman from Manhattan's Twenty-First District.

TR was surprised to get the nomination for assemblyman. He recalled, "I had at that time neither the reputation nor the ability to have won the nomination for myself, and indeed never would have thought of trying for it." If Murray had not nominated him, the course of history might have been altered.

The three years TR served as a New York state assemblyman alerted him to the corruption that ran rife in the state and taught him that fighting it could lead to political suicide. On the positive side, he learned the value of bipartisan politics. TR had to fight his battles against corruption on two fronts. He estimated that at least one third of the members of the Legislature were corrupt. As a result, he had to fight corruption from within the Legislature and among the outsiders who were trying to influence representatives to pass bills in their best interests. TR fought hard, along with a phalanx of friends from both parties, against both groups.

TR kept up the pressure against corruption on all fronts, while introducing bill after bill to establish a park in New York City, lower taxes for New Yorkers and raise them on certain businesses, strengthen laws governing child abuse, and change machine politics. Not all passed, and he did not always succeed in his reform attempts, but he never stopped trying.

The three years TR spent in the Legislature provided him with some valuable lessons about morality, chicanery, constitutionality, and political principles in general. During that time he grasped the connection between business and politics, which he later made a habit of severing. The lessons played a subsequent role in how he conducted his affairs in his politically appointed and elected positions.

Overall, the three terms he served in Albany curbed his idealism and prepared him for his later political offices at the city, state, and federal levels.

Teddy Trivia

"I put myself in the way of things happening; and they happened . . . During the three years' service in the Legislature I worked on a very simple philosophy of government. It was that personal character and initiative are the prime requisites in political and social life." – Theodore Roosevelt

FACT #24. ROOSEVELT MADE HIS FIRST POLITICAL ENEMY AT HIS FIRST CAMPAIGN STOP.

Once TR's nomination for assemblyman from his district had been made, Jake Hess, who hadn't been sure Roosevelt was ready for the nod, nevertheless joined Joe Murray in the effort to get TR elected. Once the campaign began, TR injected himself into it full bore, which was the only way he knew to accomplish something he wanted. The law degree he had sought, albeit with misgivings, was deferred—for 127 years.

But TR had no sooner entered the race than the bosses began wondering if they had created a monster.

The young candidate got off on the wrong foot with his future constituents in the early days of his first campaign. The veteran district leaders Hess and Murray accompanied TR on his campaign stops along Sixth Avenue. They thought it would be helpful for him to visit some of the tavern owners in the area, since they wielded considerable influence. The bosses quickly wished they had started somewhere else.

At the time TR began dipping his toe in politic waters, saloon-keepers in New York had cozy relationships with politicians and police officers, and bribes changed hands among them in return for licenses, special favors, and good deals with brewers—exactly the types of corrupt relationships TR wanted to end.

Hess and Murray introduced TR to saloon-keeper Valentine Young in the first tavern they entered. Mr. Young seemed a bit belligerent to TR, which he thought was strange. TR believed that as an assemblyman he would be in a position to help tavern owners. Young apparently felt that he would be telling TR what to do. That was political lesson number one for TR.

Young opined that the fees for tavern licenses were too high and that he expected TR to lower them and treat the liquor business fairly. TR informed Young that he would treat the liquor business as fairly as he treated everyone else. He was, after all, a believer in a "fair deal" for everyone. And, TR announced, he thought that liquor license fees were too low, and he would try to raise them.

Hess and Murray were aghast. They had not gotten beyond their first campaign stop and TR had already made an enemy. They hustled TR out of the tavern, escorted him over to Fifth Avenue, and advised him that they would campaign for him on Sixth Avenue. Their plan worked. TR won the election and moved to Albany.

Later, in his third year as assemblyman, TR would introduce a bill to raise liquor license fees by a large margin, a throwback to his first campaign visit to Valentine Young's saloon on Sixth Avenue, which had ended so badly. The bill failed.

Throughout his career, TR became known for siding with what he thought was right, whether that was politically expedient or not. His tussle with the saloon-keeper on Sixth Avenue was just the first of many controversies that he would engage in throughout his long political life.

FACT #25. ROOSEVELT WAS THE YOUNGEST ASSEMBLYMAN IN NEW YORK STATE'S HISTORY.

When TR started his career as an assemblyman at the tender age of twenty-three, he became the youngest legislator in the state of New York's history. He began his first term like a whirlwind, which was a harbinger of the future. Before TR ended his three years in the Assembly, he set a record for having introduced more bills into the Assembly than anyone else.

The four bills he introduced within the first forty-eight hours of his initial legislative session demonstrated his primary interests and sincerity for reform. They focused on water purification, aldermanic election reform, finance reform for New York City, and judicial reform. He learned quickly that the number of bills introduced was not important. The true measure of a legislator's effectiveness lay in the number that passed.

Only one of TR's first four bills received any attention. The Legislature passed a modified version of the aldermanic election reform bill. The numbers accomplished one thing, though. He earned some respect from a group of similar-minded independent young Republicans bent on reform and notice from a prominent *New York Times* legislative reporter, George Spinney, who decided that Roosevelt made good copy. Other journalists followed his lead.

George Spinney joined the *New York Times* staff as a legislative reporter in 1879 when it was a politically independent newspaper. In

1893, when the *Times* announced it would officially become a Democratic newspaper, an editorial writer for the *Commercial Appeal* in Memphis said, "The *Times* was originally the bitterest Republican paper in the country." That was helpful for TR in 1882.

The unofficial Republican reform group elected TR its de facto leader. With their encouragement and Spinney's news coverage, the dynamic TR began his quest to produce reform. It did not take long before TR justified their faith in finding a good story.

Despite his youth, Roosevelt impressed his constituents enough that he was re-elected as state assemblyman by a two-to-one margin in the 1882 elections. He was nominated on January 1, 1883, to stand as the Republican candidate for Assembly Speaker. Although he lost to the nominee of the majority Democrats, Roosevelt served as minority leader, quite a coup for such a young politician.

By the beginning of his second term, TR was feeling more comfortable in the Assembly. Quickly, he introduced a civil service reform bill to enhance job seekers' chances for acquiring government jobs. The legislation was modeled on a similar bill, the Pendleton Civil Service Reform Act, passed by the United States Congress in January 1883.

The Pendleton Act addressed political patronage at the federal level. It mandated that government jobs had to be awarded on the basis of merit, introduced competitive exams for civil service jobs, and made it illegal to fire or demote government employees for political reasons. The law also created the United States Civil Service Commission to enforce the mandates. That sounded about right to TR, who started his political career the way he intended to continue it: always championing for a fair deal.

Fact #26. Roosevelt's crusade against corruption started with Judge Westbrook.

Early in his tenure as New York assemblyman, TR learned about a group of high-level New York state politicians who were involved in a ring of corruption with railroad magnate Jay Gould. The politicians included the state's attorney general and Supreme Court judge Theodore Westbrook.

TR approached Republican Party leaders and asked them if they planned to address the corruption. They said they did not, and they would be happy if he did not either. Rather naively, TR vowed to do it himself.

On April 6, 1882, TR delivered a speech in the Assembly that made members of both parties cringe. He demanded that the Assembly investigate the dealings between Gould and Westbrook—and impeach the judge. The Assembly failed to act.

Roosevelt continued to convince the Assembly that it was in its best interests to end the corruption and impeach Westbrook. Veteran legislators countered that it was in his best interests to let the matter drop.

TR alleged that Judge Westbrook's rulings in a recent railroad scandal had cost legitimate investors so much money that his decisions threatened their livelihoods. He accused the judge of being a co-conspirator.

The Legislature was outraged. Newspapers picked up the story and made the legislators so uncomfortable that they were almost forced to investigate Westbrook.

TR would not back down. Day after day he spoke in the chamber about the need for an investigation. Eventually, the Legislature, spurred by the growing number of newspapers carrying stories about TR's persistence and the resulting negative publicity, voted 104 to 6 to begin an investigation.

The investigation came to nothing. There were no charges brought against Judge Westbrook. The committee that conducted the investigation delivered its findings to the Legislature, which voted 77 to 35 against impeachment.

The results disappointed TR and the citizens of New York State, but they magnified his reputation as a brash young legislator seeking reform in their best interest. He did not let up in his reform efforts.

Although TR did not accomplish all he set out to do in his first year in the Assembly, he did earn a reputation as a young politician who would not back down from anyone—including his own party leaders—in his quest for reform. Even though he had been sent to Albany to represent his district in Manhattan, he was there to fight for all New Yorkers.

The voters of his district were supportive of TR after his first year's performance. They re-elected him in 1882, expecting more of the same from him. He did not disappoint them.

TR began his second year in a stronger power position in the Assembly. The Republicans put forth his name for the Assembly speakership.

Since the Democrats held a majority, he became the minority leader. Regardless of his position in the Assembly, he continued to pursue reform, which he knew many of his colleagues opposed.

In his January 26, 1883, speech at Buffalo, New York, "The Duties of American Citizenship," TR said, "Nothing is more effective in thwarting the purposes of the spoilsmen than the civil service reform. To be sure, practical politicians sneer at it." He considered himself practical, but he never sneered at reform, civil or otherwise.

Teddy Trivia

In the late 1860s, railroad developer Jay Gould named Tammany Hall boss William Tweed a director of the Erie Railroad. In return, Tweed arranged favorable legislation for him. That irritated the citizens of New York, but the state Legislature did not address the resulting corruption. Gould also had a controlling interest in the New York City elevated railroads after 1881.

FACT #27. ROOSEVELT WORKED WITH THE DEMOCRATIC GOVERNOR OF NEW YORK, GROVER CLEVELAND, TO PASS LEGISLATION TO ROOT OUT CORRUPTION.

One of TR's strongest allies in enacting his proposed legislation was the New York State governor, Grover Cleveland. The two men formed an unholy and unpopular alliance early in Cleveland's tenure, even though TR was a Republican and Cleveland was a Democrat.

Despite their differences in political philosophy, Roosevelt and Cleveland were both committed to honest, efficient government. Cleveland privately discussed strategy with Roosevelt and publicly endorsed The New York State version of the Pendleton Act, which passed both houses and was signed into law in May 1883.

Another early 1883 bill that highlighted the connection between Cleveland and Roosevelt reduced fares on New York City's elevated trains from ten cents to a nickel. Jay Gould had instituted the increases in an effort to make the city's failing railway system solvent. The legislators, including TR, voted to reverse the hikes, because Gould was unpopular. The governor vetoed the bill—one of eight vetoes he delivered in his first two months in office.

The governor's veto was as unpopular among legislators as Gould. Yet, he had a valid reason for vetoing the bill. He believed it was unjust, since the fee hike was necessary. Cleveland also argued that legislatively changing Gould's franchise violated the contract clause of the U.S. Constitution. Newspapers sided with the governor.

The governor's veto convinced TR to take a second look at the bill. He acknowledged voting for it originally even though he believed it was wrong. But he voted for it more to punish Gould than anything else. After careful consideration, he realized that Cleveland was right. He voted to sustain the veto, which the Legislature sustained. The governor had taught him a valuable lesson: People's first impressions are not always the right ones.

Later, the Cigar Makers' Union introduced a bill into the Legislature seeking to ban the manufacture of cigars in tenements. TR was appointed to a three-member committee to investigate the conditions in the tenements. He learned a valuable lesson about the role of political influence in legislations. One other member of the committee said he had to vote for the bill because he represented labor interests. A second said his orders were to vote against it because he represented businesses. But he told TR he did not care personally one way or the other which way the vote went.

After studying the bill—including visiting the tenements where cigars were made—TR decided to support the bill. At TR's urging, Governor Cleveland signed it. Ultimately, a Court of Appeals declared the bill unconstitutional, much to TR's chagrin.

The Court of Appeals based its decision on the fact that one home in which the cigars were made was an ideal spot for the process. They labeled the law an assault upon the "hallowed" influences of "home." The outcome of the case taught TR "the courts were not necessarily the best judges of what should be done to better social and industrial conditions."

TR said later that this decision completely blocked tenement-house reform legislation in New York for at least twenty years. In fact, he emphasized, it was one of the most serious setbacks the cause of industrial and social progress and reform had ever received.

But, as so often happened in TR's case, the setback turned into a victory of sorts. He learned more about playing the political game and impressed Governor Cleveland. The two would work together closely again, despite their different political affiliations.

FACT #28. ROOSEVELT AND CLEVELAND BECAME TAMMANY HALLS'S "CO-ENEMIES NUMBER ONE."

TR was elected to a third term in the 1883 election. His constituents still supported him. The Republican Party did not. They conspired to remove him from any leadership position in 1884 because he was stepping on too many toes. That did not stop him. As a consolation prize, the leaders appointed him to the Cities Committee. That worked in his favor.

Democrats and Republicans alike looked to TR for floor leadership in the Assembly. He ended up with more power than he would have had as the official House leader and learned a valuable lesson from the situation. He commented, "As so often, I found that the titular position was of no consequence; what counted was the combination of the opportunity with the ability to accomplish results."

TR's 1883 re-election victory as assemblyman gave him the opportunity to change the role of the aldermen in New York City. He deemed it the most important challenge of the term. TR saw it as a chance to get the citizens of the city involved in politics to their benefit.

In the mid-1880s, aldermen in New York City had the power of confirmation over the mayor's appointments. The real power lay in the hands of the ward bosses, who controlled the aldermen. TR and his allies in the

Assembly believed that if they could reduce the aldermen's power, they would eliminate a critical step in the appointment process and give ordinary citizens a stronger voice.

The appointment to the Cities Committee opened the door for him to pursue the reform he thought was so badly needed in New York City. The 1884 session had no sooner started than TR introduced a bill into the Assembly that got him and Governor Cleveland into hot water again— on the same side.

The Reform Charter Bill, as it was called, upset the political machine leaders in New York City because its intent was to weaken them and to increase citizens' chances of electing a reform mayor. That intrigued Governor Cleveland, who had been elected largely on his strength as a reformer. His support of TR's bill drew the ire of Tammany Hall, which supported aldermanic chicanery. The battle lines were drawn once again.

There was a definite need for aldermanic reform in 1884. Several members of the Board of Aldermen were involved in a scheme to help entrepreneur Jake Sharp acquire a Broadway railroad franchise at a noncompetitive price. In exchange, they received kickbacks (called "boodles") and acquired the nickname "The Boodle Board."

TR delivered an eloquent speech to support passage of the Reform Charter Bill that drew praise from almost every newspaper in New York. The bill passed, and he and Governor Cleveland became Tammany Hall's "Co-Enemies Number One." That did not bother either man. It simply demonstrated that they were accomplishing what they were elected to do: enact civil reform.

Teddy Trivia

The Tammany Society began as a patriotic and charitable organization in New York City in 1789. In 1798, Aaron Burr transformed it into a political organization. Eventually, Irish immigrants seized control, and trading votes for benefits became a standard practice. When William Tweed took over in 1868, he began a statewide reign of extreme corruption that lasted into the early 1900s.

FACT #29. AFTER HIS THIRD YEAR AS AN ASSEMBLYMAN, ROOSEVELT TOOK TIME OFF FROM POLITICS.

As TR's third term in office ended, he became embroiled in one more controversy that involved Grover Cleveland indirectly. Again, TR did not endear himself to his party.

TR was selected as a delegate to the Republican National Convention in Chicago in 1884. Then-president Chester Arthur (who had become president after James A. Garfield was assassinated) was seeking the Republican Party nomination. Instead, the party nominated James G. Blaine as its candidate. Blaine was the leader of the "Half Breed" faction of the Republican Party. The "Half Breed" party was a reformist party—many members of the faction had called for civil service reform in the form of merit appointments (versus patronage appointments). Ironically,

Blaine had a reputation for being corrupt. Specifically, he was accused of graft and corruption in the granting of railroad charters in the late 1800s, which earned him nicknames like "The Continental Liar from the State of Maine" and "Slippery Jim."

TR opposed the nomination, as did many other Republicans. One of them was George William Curtis, an ardent reformer of the civil service at the federal level, who noted in a statement after the convention ended that TR would play a major role in politics in the future.

A faction pushed for the party to back the Democratic candidate, Grover Cleveland. TR refused their entreaties to join them. As much as he had enjoyed working with Cleveland in New York, he could not break from his party and campaign for a Democrat. The incident shook his idealism in the political process.

The prescient Curtis had this to say about the young Theodore Roosevelt:

> *Later the nation will be criticizing or praising him. While respectful to the gray hairs and experience of his elders, none of them can move him an iota from convictions as to men and measures once formed and rooted. He has integrity, courage, fair scholarship, a love for public life, a comfortable amount of money, honorable descent, the good word of the honest. He will not truckle nor cringe, he seems to court opposition to the point of being somewhat pugnacious. His political life will probably be a turbulent one, but he will be a figure, not a figurehead, in future development—or, if not, it will be because he gives up politics altogether.*

Curtis was right on all points. Despite his success as an assembly-man, TR grew disillusioned with politics and radically changed career paths, albeit temporarily. It was another two years before he ran for office again.

TR's decision to take some time off from politics was not due entirely to his experiences in the Legislature or at the National Convention in Chicago. His self-imposed respite was hastened by a personal tragedy: the death of his wife, Alice Hathaway Lee, on February 14, 1884.

FACT #30. ROOSEVELT'S WIFE ALICE DIED ON VALENTINE'S DAY IN 1884, JUST AFTER GIVING BIRTH TO THEIR DAUGHTER.

When TR began his third term in the Legislature, Alice was both pregnant and ill. That put pressure on him. But there was added work-related stress he had to contend with as his term began. TR was facing opposition from his own party as he struggled to become the Speaker of the Assembly. While he was in Albany looking for votes, a series of notes and telegrams arrived that sent him scurrying back to New York City.

Only six days before his daughter was born, TR wrote to Alice in a letter, "How did I hate to leave my bright, sunny little love yesterday afternoon! I love you and long for you all the time, and oh so tenderly; doubly tenderly now, my sweetest little wife. I just long for Friday evening when I shall be with you again." He did see her shortly, but not under the circumstances he imagined.

Alice sent TR a note on February 11 to assure him that she was fine and that the doctor was not particularly concerned about her health. Next, she sent him a telegram to announce that they had a daughter, who was born on February 12. Then, he received a telegram advising him to return to New York City immediately because Alice's health was deteriorating. There, a terrible double tragedy and a moment of joy awaited him. They did not offset one another in his thinking.

When TR arrived at his house on February 13, he walked into a scene of utter despair. His mother Mittie was dying of typhoid fever in one room; one floor above, Alice was fighting for her life from complications of childbirth and Bright's disease.

There was little that TR could do except shuffle from room to room in a futile vigil for two of the most cherished women in his life.

Alice fought until she drew her last breath in TR's arms at about 2 P.M. that day. It was a bitter anniversary for TR. Not only was it Valentine's Day, but it was the fourth anniversary of his engagement to Alice. It was of little comfort to TR, but at least he was there to hold her as she died.

A few days after Alice died in 1884, TR expressed in his diary his fond memories of the three years they had together: "We spent three years of happiness greater and more unalloyed than I have ever known to fall to the lot of others."

TR was devastated. Two entries in his diary showed his anguish. In one, he wrote a large X and a solitary sentence stating, "The light has gone out of my life." Alice's death left him with a large void that he sought to fill in the only way he knew how: work.

In a second entry, he wrote, "On February 17th I christened the baby Alice Lee Roosevelt. For joy or for sorrow my life has now been lived out."

Teddy Trivia

Alice's death was attributed to Bright's disease, a kidney ailment. Today, it is known as acute or chronic nephritis. Sadly, it might have been treatable under ordinary circumstances. In Alice's case, her pregnancy masked the symptoms.

FACT #31. ROOSEVELT'S MOTHER DIED ON THE SAME DAY AS HIS WIFE.

Mittie and Alice Hathaway Lee Roosevelt passed away within hours of each other on February 14, 1884. Alice was twenty-two years old at the time. Mittie was relatively young, too. She was forty-eight. Mittie died first, at approximately 3 A.M.

The family buried Alice and Mittie at a double funeral on February 15, 1884. The women were laid to rest together in Greenwood Cemetery. The epitaph on Alice's grave reads, "For joy or for sorrow my life has now been lived out."

Both of TR's parents had come from aristocratic families. His mother's family was included on the list of wealthy, elite Georgia planters. They established a pattern for their children, which included formal and informal schooling and field training.

TR downplayed the influence his mother played in his life. He said that she was a "sweet, gracious, beautiful Southern woman, a delightful companion and beloved by everybody." She was a most devoted mother with a great sense of humor, he recalled, but for the most part it was his father from whom he learned the most in life.

One memory TR had about his mother's sense of humor revolved around her Civil War Southern loyalty. She disciplined him one day, unjustly in his opinion. As retribution, he prayed loudly that night in her presence for the Union's success in the war. She laughed and warned him not to do that again, lest she tell his father. He heeded her advice, and Thee did not learn about the incident.

TR overlooked the role she played in his life as he grew older, especially when he went to college. She did not want TR living on campus with the other students, which created some uncomfortable moments for him. Many of his classmates found it a bit odd that one of their peers was so pampered and antisocial.

There was a fine line between protection and overprotection in their view. His mother crossed that line. It was just one more obstacle that TR had to overcome in his struggle to become independent and accepted. That helps explain why he gave more credit to his father than his mother for molding him into a productive member of society who could stand on his own two feet.

Many years later TR delivered a speech to the National Congress of Mothers in Washington, D.C., on March 13, 1905, that showed the importance of mothers to him—perhaps both Alice and Mittie influenced his talk. It was no secret that he was sympathetic to the status of women and children in society. As he wrote in a later book, *The Conservation of Womanhood and Childhood*, published in 1912, "We must work then for each partial remedy that may alleviate something of the misery of mankind, that may cause a measurable betterment in the condition of children, women and men."

FACT #32. ROOSEVELT TRIED TO ERASE ALL MEMORY OF ALICE, INCLUDING NEVER SPEAKING OF HER AGAIN.

In a way, TR's reaction to the deaths of his mother and his wife on the same day was out of the ordinary. He tried to erase his memories of Alice by destroying any photographs and all correspondence that made any reference to her. He vowed to never speak of her again, even to her namesake and his daughter. For the most part, he managed not to.

TR even declared that he did not want to hear the name "Teddy" again.

TR's refusal to talk about Alice deprived the world of a great deal of knowledge about the happy life they lived together. (Her name is not even mentioned in his autobiography.) But there was a major obstacle to forgetting Alice Hathaway Lee Roosevelt altogether: his newborn daughter, Alice. Everyone took to calling her "Baby Lee" so as to avoid using the name "Alice." Later in life she went by "Mrs. L."

TR broke his self-enforced rule not to speak of Alice Hathaway Lee Roosevelt after her death. He wrote of her in a private moment:

> *She was beautiful in face and form, and lovelier still in spirit; As a flower she grew, and as a fair young flower she died. Her life had been always in the sunshine; there had never come to her a single sorrow; and none ever knew her who did not love and revere her for the bright, sunny temper and her saintly unselfishness. Fair, pure, and joyous as a maiden; loving, tender, and happy. As a young wife; when she had just become a mother, when her life seemed to be just begun, and when the years seemed so bright before her—then, by a strange and terrible fate, death came to her. And when my heart's dearest died, the light went from my life forever.*

Well, perhaps not forever. In 1884, after his wife died, he moved to the Dakota Territory (which he had visited and liked in 1883) for two years in order to forget her. TR bought two ranches and immersed himself in the Western lifestyle. He learned a great deal about people's ability to adapt to new circumstances and mended himself mentally, physically, and spiritually. After a disastrous winter ruined his business venture, TR returned to New York with a much healthier attitude about the western United States—and a renewed zeal for life.

TR's daughter led an unconventional and rebellious—possibly one could say "notorious"—life, which was attributed by some to TR's refusal to speak to her of her mother. Their relationship was not always easy, although Alice did support him in his later political career (when others did not). Coincidentally, Alice's daughter, Paulina, was born on February 14, 1925. It was the forty-first anniversary of Alice Hathaway Lee Roosevelt's death. Scandalously, Alice's husband, the representative Nicholas Longworth, was not Paulina's father. The real father was U.S. Senator William Borah of Idaho.

FACT #33. ROOSEVELT'S SISTER TOOK OVER THE CHALLENGE OF RAISING HIS DAUGHTER ALICE.

After the death of his wife, the grief-stricken TR asked his sister Bamie to care for his daughter. Bamie had to walk a tightrope with regard to Alice Hathaway Lee Roosevelt's death and TR's refusal to speak publicly of her or let anyone mention her name in his presence. Young Alice did ask him occasionally about her mother, but he always referred her to Bamie. As a result, Alice learned about her mother from her aunt, who became her confidante.

While Bamie took over the task of raising young Alice, TR sought a way to forget his beloved wife. His way of coping was to erase her memory completely, an impossibility. Her memory would follow him wherever he went. Nevertheless, he tried to escape it.

Not long after the funerals of Alice and his mother, he took another step in his quest to try to forget Alice: TR left New York (and his infant daughter).

The light may have gone out of his life, but it would come back on eventually. It began to gleam again in the Dakota Badlands, where he took up ranching for a time. A few years later, TR married again. That created the vexing problem of what to do about baby Alice, who was now three. TR wanted to let Bamie raise her. His new wife Edith did not. She wanted Alice to be part of their family.

In the end, Alice came to live with the newlywed couple shortly after they began their married life. Again, Bamie's steady influence played a role in the decision, as it did so often in TR's life. She helped them resolve their dilemma over what to do about Alice. Bamie turned young Alice over to them in May of 1887, although it broke her heart to do so.

Alice did not always fit well into the family structure. There was friction between TR and Alice from the beginning. Bamie had done a sound job raising her while TR was in the Badlands trying to forget the child's mother. Even though TR's new wife had gladly consented to raise Alice as her own, there was always a wall between them.

Years later, after Alice got married at the White House on February 17, 1906, Edith sent her off with some less than friendly words. According to Stacy A. Cordery, author of a biography of Alice Roosevelt Longworth, Edith said, "I want you to know I am glad to see you leave. You have never been anything but trouble."

TR did not live to see the type of life Alice led after she left the White House. He did hear, however, one of her quips about a major episode in his life. She and her husband, Ohio representative Nicholas Longworth, went to Cuba for their honeymoon. They visited Kettle Hill (San Juan Hill), where TR had led his famous charge in 1898. She said she found the hill "mildly sloping."

PART 4

A New Start

Fact #34. In 1884, Roosevelt moved to the Dakota Territory, trying to escape memories of his dead wife.

TR had been living a rather sedentary life between his graduation from Harvard and his trip to the Badlands. Once he bought his ranch there, he pursued the "strenuous life" again.

TR was happy living the hard life of a cowboy. He made it sound at times like a life of ease and downplayed the work that went into surviving the rigors of the West. He said about his time in the Territory: "It was a fine, healthy life, too; it taught a man self-reliance, hardihood, and the value of instant decision—in short, the virtues that ought to come from life in the open country. I enjoyed the life to the full."

Two of TR's old guides from Maine responded to his request to help him manage the Elkhorn Ranch. William W. Sewall and his nephew Wilmot Dow, neither of whom had any experience working with cattle or ranches, joined him in 1884. Their wives and children arrived shortly thereafter—and practically drove TR out of his own home. Both women gave birth to children there in 1886, which kept the house abuzz with activity at times.

Part of his satisfaction was the hard work. Another part was the companionship. TR's cattle herd survived the winter of 1883–1884 with no problems. The success of his venture may have lured him into a false sense of security. He acquired his second ranch, the Elkhorn, for only $400 and invited some of his friends from "Back East" to join him there. The value of choosing the right friends paid off once again.

TR discovered cattle ranching at a time when it was becoming popular in the Dakota Territory. During the 1885–1886 season, he owned between 3,000 and 5,000 cattle. He became so involved in the operation that he helped organize the Little Missouri River Stockmen's Association. Eventually, he became its chairman and then president. He was also a member of the Montana Stockgrowers Association. His life was going well, but disaster lay ahead.

While his friends built new buildings and managed the herds on his two ranches, TR settled into the rigorous life of the Badlands and insinuated himself into the local life. The Elkhorn became his "home" ranch.

TR continued to write while he was at his ranches. He completed *Hunting Trips of a Ranchman* at the Maltese Cross Ranch in 1885 and almost finished *Life of Thomas Hart Benton* the following year at the Elkhorn Ranch. He found it difficult to stay away from his writing, no matter how many cattle had to be fed.

No matter where he was, TR impressed everyone with his willingness to work hard, his ability to pick up the tricks of the cowboy trade, the rapidity with which he adapted to the life, and his transformation from a thin, "four eyed," raw Easterner into a healthy, robust man.

Teddy Trivia

"It was still the Wild West in those days, the Far West of Owen Wister's stories, and Frederic Remington's drawings, the soldier and the cowpuncher. The land of the West has gone now, 'gone, gone with the lost Atlantis,' gone to the isle of ghosts and strange

dead memories . . . In that land we led a hardy life. Ours was the glory of work and the
joy of living." – Theodore Roosevelt

Fact #35. Roosevelt first visited the Dakota Territory in 1883, looking for buffalo to hunt.

TR's 1884 trip to erase the memories of his deceased wife was not his first
visit to the Dakota Territory. He had been there earlier under happier circumstances, most recently in 1883, when Alice was pregnant and he was
looking for some diversion.

TR arrived in the Dakota Territory for the first time before dawn at the
Little Missouri train depot on September 8, 1883. The timing was hardly aus-
picious. TR had left his beloved wife at home; he did not know anyone in the
Badlands—and he did not have a horse. None of those factors bothered him.

One thing TR had in his favor was a pocket full of cash, which he
used to induce Joe Ferris, a twenty-five-year-old hunting guide from New
Brunswick, Canada, to help him. The rugged individualists in North
Dakota may have distrusted Easterners in general, but they did respect
the value of a dollar.

Conditions were not suitable for buffalo hunting in western North
Dakota in September 1883 as the men set off on the hunt. (Buffalo are
known technically as bison, a distinction TR's naturalist side would
appreciate.) The weather was rainy and commercial hunters had practically eliminated any buffalo in the territory.

Despite the difficulty TR had in finding live buffalo, he put his time to good use. He and Ferris spent their evenings at the ranch managed for Sir John Pender by Gregor Lang, a recent immigrant from Scotland. While Ferris recovered from the relentless pace of each day's hunt, TR peppered Lang with questions about ranching, life in the West, and politics. Lang's answers intrigued TR. He decided to buy a ranch of his own. First he had to find a buffalo to shoot.

Determination had always been one of TR's strongest characteristics. He had traveled to North Dakota to shoot a buffalo, and he wasn't going to leave without one. It took almost a week of hunting in steady rain, but he finally succeeded.

TR shot an old bull, which was one of only 1,200 buffalo left in the world. Virtually all the rest were killed by the end of 1884. TR's kill left him with just one more goal before returning to New York: buying a ranch.

TR, not one to pass up what he considered to be a wise investment, offered to buy the herd Lang managed. Lang demurred and suggested that TR approach Sylvane Ferris and William Merrifield, who were running the Maltese Cross Ranch for a Minnesota-based company named Wadsworth and Hawley. The three men agreed to a fairly complicated contract that was signed in St. Paul, Minnesota, on September 27, 1883.

According to the terms, Ferris and Merrifield agreed to manage up to 400 cattle on the ranch for seven years at a cost to TR of no more than $12,000. (Some accounts suggest that he paid $14,000 initially.) At the end of the seven years, Ferris and Merrifield would return to TR 400 cattle or their equivalent in value.

If there were any increases in the number of cattle during that period, Ferris and Merrifield would receive half of them. The contract permitted TR to add cattle according to the same terms as the initial 400 animals. The timing was propitious for him, but the venture ended in disaster several years later.

TR returned to New York, where he was re-elected to the state assembly. Dakota Territory became a memory until Alice died.

Fact #36. Roosevelt became a deputy sheriff during his time in the Dakota Territory.

TR learned quickly that a rancher's profits could be crimped by rustlers, horse thieves, claim jumpers, and other criminals, but the West was generally safer than the East. He opined that, "A man has very little more to fear in the West than in the East, in spite of all the lawless acts one reads about." But he did not leave law enforcement to chance. TR became a lawman—a deputy sheriff. He demonstrated respect for the law rather than giving thieves a fair trial and then hanging them.

TR served as a deputy sheriff for the northern end of Billings County at a time when shootings, stabbings, stealing cattle, and other serious crimes were on the decline. The job did not carry with it a great deal of prestige—or pay. Deputy sheriffs were paid when they made arrests and received travel reimbursement. On a couple notable occasions TR earned considerable amounts of prestige and pay for his exploits.

Law enforcement work taught TR a valuable lesson that he applied to other aspects of his life. It was not an epiphany for him. He had been aware since childhood that he had limitations, especially in the physical arena. The trick, he learned, was to act first and outsmart his opponents.

For example, TR arrested several miscreants who were stronger than him and quicker with weapons. In such cases, he thought ahead and acted faster than the criminal. That prevented him from becoming the victim of physical violence and saved him from the embarrassment of finishing second best in confrontations. TR was a firm believer in the adage "He who hesitates is lost."

On one occasion in March 1886, TR, Sewall, and Dow pursued three "bad guys" who had stolen the only boat they had on the ranch. Sewall and Dow quickly built another boat and the chase began. They apprehended the thieves after a harrowing adventure.

The three men did not receive a great deal of reward for their effort. According to TR, "Under the laws of Dakota I received my fees as a deputy sheriff for making the three arrests, and also mileage for the three hundred odd miles gone over—a total of some fifty dollars." That was small compensation for time lost and wear and tear on their equipment.

But TR was not as much interested in the reward as he was in applying justice. That did not change whether he was in New York or North Dakota.

TR's career as a deputy sheriff did not occupy a lot of his time. He spent most of his time running his ranches, with the able assistance of his friends and coworkers. They gave him the time to hunt, learn the trade of "cowboying," and fraternize with the hardy people who populated the West and for whom he formed an everlasting romantic picture that he never forgot.

Teddy Trivia

The journalist Jacob Riis recounted one story that demonstrated TR's respect for law and justice. Local ranchers believed that their sheriff was sympathetic to cattle rustlers, some of whom he had let escape. The ranchers would not confront him. TR did. At one meeting, he accused the sheriff directly of favoring the outlaws and informed him that he had lost the ranchers' confidence and good will. The sheriff did not even defend himself.

FACT #37. DISASTROUS WEATHER DESTROYED ROOSEVELT'S RANCHES IN THE DAKOTA TERRITORY.

As much as TR liked the Badlands, he did not spend all his time there. He returned to New York in the winter to work on various projects that he had let slip while hunting and ranching.

On one of his trips back East, TR met an old friend of his, Edith Carow, with whom he formed a romantic attachment. That changed any plans he had to settle permanently in the West—if he had ever had any.

The problem actually began in the spring of 1886, with a late thaw. The summer temperatures rose as high as 125 degrees, which impacted plant growth. These were ominous signs for the ranchers. To compound matters, there were too many cattle on the land. Overgrazing was affecting the herds adversely. Disaster was a step or two away.

All the signs that the winter of 1886–1887 was going to be devastating to the Dakota Territory cattle industry proved true. Blizzards raged across the plains; cattle froze to death everywhere. The ranchers could not feed them.

TR returned from his honeymoon trip to Europe in the spring of 1887 and traveled to Medora to check on his cattle. He discovered that more than half of them had died during the winter. He also lost more than half of the $80,000 he had invested. He could not tolerate any more losses.

Even though his Western adventure ended badly, TR returned home with fond memories and new ideas. He made up his mind to apply some of those new ideas whenever the right situations arose.

He also learned the value of friendship and loyalty. TR crossed paths often in later years with people he met and worked with in the West. Sometimes he helped them; other times they helped him.

Perhaps the biggest lesson TR learned in his brief stay in the West was the need for conservation. He had experienced reservations about the overstocking of cattle and the resulting overgrazing in the Dakota Territory ever since his arrival—although that did not stop him from investing. His fears were realized in the winter of 1886–1887 when the lack of food for cattle and the harsh weather almost destroyed the ranching industry there.

TR realized that there had to be a balance between human and animal needs and nature's ability to provide for them. The search for that balance became one of his focal issues later in the various political and government offices he filled.

There was a lot of pressure on TR to return to New York City for good. There was no point in staying in the Dakota Territory, since his cattle were all but gone and rebuilding his herds would be costly. Besides, with a new wife and a call from politicians to get him to run for mayor of New York, he did not see a future in the Badlands.

TR opted to return to the home of his birth. He had matured mentally and physically during his hiatus in the West. For him, leaving the land he had learned to love was simply closing another chapter in his book of life. The city and the state of New York—and ultimately the United States—would benefit from his return.

FACT #38. IN 1885, ROOSEVELT BECAME ENGAGED TO HIS CHILDHOOD FRIEND, EDITH KERMIT CAROW.

Not long after Alice's death, TR met his childhood friend Edith ("Edie") Kermit Carow at his sister's house. It was not long before "Teedie" and "Edie" became romantically involved, as many people had suspected they would when they were younger.

On November 17, 1885, TR proposed to Edith. She accepted. But he did not make their betrothal public at first. He was afraid that people would think he had not allowed enough time to get over his first marriage. But it was not like he was falling head over heels for someone he did not know. Even so, TR caught a lot of people off guard, especially close family members, when he announced his engagement to Edith.

It was understandable, given the social mores of the period, that TR was reluctant to marry a second time, especially so soon after Alice's untimely death. But, Edith Kermit Carow's charms were too alluring for him to ignore.

TR and Edith were married in a small wedding with few guests at St. George's Church, Hanover Square, in London on December 2, 1886. Britain's future ambassador to the United States during World War I, Cecil Spring-Rice, was TR's best man. That was the first day of a long and happy marriage for Edith and TR.

The newlyweds stayed in Europe for their fifteen-week honeymoon. TR, ever the romantic and adventurer, took the opportunity to lead a group to the top of Mont Blanc, the highest mountain in the Alps. The British Royal Society was so impressed with his achievement that it inducted him into its ranks, which was a significant honor.

TR was a little careful in where they went, what they did, and who they saw on the honeymoon. He did not want to go places that he and first wife Alice had visited together, since his memories of her were still strong. Nevertheless, they traveled extensively and cavorted with a wide range of people, especially in England.

Cecil Spring-Rice, or "Springy," as TR called him, opened doors for the Roosevelts. TR spent large blocks of time at exclusive social clubs like the Athenaeum and St. James, which was noted as a gathering place for traveling diplomats. He socialized with political and literary figures such as the poet Robert Browning; Sir James Bryce, a member of the British Parliament at the time; and George Otto Trevelyan, a noted statesman, historian, and writer.

The social contacts were beneficial to TR, especially in the case of Bryce, who was appointed in 1907 as the British ambassador to the United States during TR's first full term as president. The Roosevelts were often weekend guests at country houses around the nation.

TR and Edith spent the winter months on the Riviera and then traveled to Italy, where they visited Milan, Rome, Venice, and Florence. In Florence, reality struck. It was there that they heard about the terrible blizzards that had devastated the Badlands while they were frolicking in Europe.

Teddy Trivia

On their wedding day, the fog swirling throughout the church was so thick that the bride and groom had difficulty picking each other out in the crowd. TR wore a pair of bright orange gloves so Edith could identify him, lest she marry the wrong man. Fog notwithstanding, the ceremony went on and the honeymoon, which lasted for thirty-three years, began. She obviously did not marry the wrong man.

Fact #39. Despite Edith's disapproval, Roosevelt ran for mayor of New York City in 1886 (and lost).

Theodore had no sooner returned from North Dakota when he got the political itch again and campaigned for mayor of New York City in 1886. He had some significant opposition: the Tammany Hall nominee Democrat Abram S. Hewitt; Henry George, economist and reformer, who had moved to New York City from California a few years earlier; and Edith.

She may not have been on the ticket, but Edith was against TR's involvement based on two issues: They were planning a wedding in Europe less than a month after Election Day, and he would have to take office only a few weeks after that if he won, which would cut into their honeymoon. Despite her objections, TR ran—and lost. At least he did not lose Edith.

The race was an eye-opener for TR. His opponents overshadowed him and his supporters practically ignored him. He understood that, and he did not expect to win. He was scheduled to sail to Europe with Edith only four days after the election.

TR was right about the outcome of the election, but he had no intention of leaving politics. Many people believed that someone like TR, who came from one of the city's aristocratic families, should not be involved in politics. What could he know about the severe economic depression, high levels of unemployment, political graft, and labor disorders that were plaguing the city, they wondered? As a result, many Republicans crossed party lines and voted for his opponents. Perhaps that was for the best as far as TR's career was concerned.

Almost all the city's aldermen were under indictment for taking bribes; workers were extremely underpaid for the long hours they toiled—sometimes as many as sixteen hours a day—and labor unions were agitating for power.

Hewitt represented the most powerful political machine in New York—and the United States. He was a seasoned campaigner who had served five terms in the U.S. House of Representatives. (He resigned during his fifth term to take over his mayoral duties.) Strangely enough, he shared some characteristics with TR that George could not emulate.

Hewitt, like TR, was rich and a philanthropist. That helped him, but it worked against TR. Hewitt had worked his way to millionaire status starting with a public school background, whereas TR had been born with the proverbial silver spoon in his mouth. In truth, by 1886 TR's personal wealth was nowhere near Hewitt's.

In the long run, Hewitt's age (he was sixty-four years old), government experience, family connections, ties to a political machine, and promise that he was the only candidate who could save New York City from "socialism, communism, anarchism, nihilism, and revolution" were too much for TR to overcome.

TR campaigned enthusiastically, but lost badly in the November 2, 1886, election. He placed a distant third behind runner-up Henry George. There was one consolation: He did not finish last. That honor went to Prohibition Party candidate William T. Wardwell.

No doubt the results of the race elicited a sigh of relief from Edith. They did not faze TR. He commented simply, "Well, anyway, I had a bully time." The loss provided him with valuable experience that he would use in later years and freed him to make wedding plans with Edith.

Teddy Trivia

There were 219,992 votes cast in the 1886 New York City mayoral election. The breakdown, according to the November 14, 1886, *New York Times*: Hewitt (90,552); George (68,110); Roosevelt (60,435); Wardwell (582). The final tally left 313 votes unaccounted for, but the missing votes were not enough to sway the outcome.

FACT #40. MANY PEOPLE CONSIDERED EDITH A BETTER JUDGE OF MONEY AND MEN THAN HER HUSBAND.

Edith and TR established a pattern in their home that would persist through their years of marriage. Edith managed the house and the budget well, particularly in light of TR's reduced income due to the loss of his cattle. She did it so well that she managed to buy a house for him without his knowledge once they moved to Washington, D.C., and he became president.

Many people considered Edith to be a better judge than TR of men and of money. They needed that balance, because of his lack of money management skills and his overall joy of life, which tended to cost him a few dollars here and there. Her money management and social skills served them in good stead as the number of Roosevelts increased at Sagamore Hill and beyond.

The experience Edith gained dealing with limited financial resources came into play after they were married. She and TR had both learned a valuable lesson based on her family's setbacks and the losses he had incurred after the Badlands disaster. They kept tighter reins on their own finances once the honeymoon ended.

Edith was no stranger to dwindling resources. Her own family, although affluent prior to the Civil War, suffered severe financial setbacks afterward due to inflation and her father's alcoholism. Their fortunes were reversed badly enough by 1867 that the Carows could not afford their own home. They lived with relatives, but their social standing remained intact.

TR's letters to his children are filled with pieces of advice regarding success, how to achieve it, and what he expected of them. He was accomplishing two purposes through the letters: expanding on the advice handed down to him and integrating it with his own experiences.

He mentioned Edith often, but as a sort of postscript. "Mother has gone off for nine days . . ." "Mother and I have just come home from a lovely trip to Pine Knot . . ." "Mother was away [so] I made a point of seeing the children each evening for three-quarters of an hour or so . . ." It was a throwback to his own upbringing: "Mother" was in the background, while "Father" dispensed the advice to the children.

But, that was TR: always in charge—except when Edith took a page out of his book and made decisions such as buying Pine Knot, introducing innovations in the White House, and deciding when he needed a vacation.

Regardless of whom he was writing to, and what the subject was, one thing shone through: TR was a proud father overseeing a mostly happy family.

Teddy Trivia

TR may have been deluding himself at times about who was in charge. In an April 30, 1906, letter to Kermit, he wrote: "On Saturday afternoon Mother and I started off . . . Mother having made up her mind I needed thirty-six hours' rest, and we had a delightful time together, and she was just as cunning as she could be." Edith suggested; TR obeyed.

FACT #41. ROOSEVELT'S FIRST CHILD WITH EDITH WAS BORN IN 1887 AND THEIR LAST (THE FIFTH) IN 1897.

The couple did not waste any time starting a family. They already had one child, Alice, from TR's first marriage. Their own first child, Theodore Jr., was born on September 13, 1887, at Sagamore Hill. Kermit followed two years later, on October 10, 1889, also at Sagamore Hill. Their third child, Ethel Carow, arrived on August 13, 1891.

As TR accepted new responsibilities and assignments, the family moved to fit their circumstances. Archibald Bulloch was born in Washington, D.C., on April 9, 1894. Quentin followed him on November 19, 1897. He was the couple's final child. They all made TR happy, although they were not without problems.

Edith had several miscarriages between children. But he and Edith bore up well under the strains of managing a career and raising children, as he averred time and time again in the book, *Theodore Roosevelt's Letters to His Children*. One letter in particular, written on December 26, 1903, to his sister Corinne (Mrs. Douglas Robinson), displayed how emotional he could be about family relationships, as a boy himself and a father:

> *We had a delightful Christmas yesterday—just such a Christmas thirty or forty years ago we used to have under Father's and Mother's supervision in 20th Street and 57th street . . . I wonder whether there ever can come in life a thrill of greater exaltation and rapture than that which comes to one between the ages of say six and fourteen, when the library door is thrown open and you walk in to see all the gifts, like a materialized fairy land, arrayed on your special table?*

In the final analysis, the two major losses in TR's life between February 14, 1884, and November 2, 1886, turned out to be positive events. As heartbroken as TR was over the death of Alice Hathaway Lee, he rebounded magnificently. His subsequent marriage to Edith Carow turned out to be one of the happiest relationships of his life.

The blow he suffered in losing the 1886 mayoral race contributed to the beginning and enduring strength of that relationship. Moreover, it served as a positive experience for him.

TR learned that losing a political race is no disgrace as long as you treat it as a teachable moment, apply the lessons you learned, and move on. He did just that. Together, he, Edith, and their children moved on and up.

Even though the Roosevelt family life seemed "Edenesque" at times, there were a few of the proverbial skeletons in the closet endemic to most families. Alice may have been a disappointment at times to TR. So was Kermit, who committed suicide on June 4, 1943, after struggling with alcoholism and depression. That, too, occurred after TR's death. Only one of his children, Quentin, died before he did. He died a hero's death. Quentin was just one hero among many in the Roosevelt family.

FACT #42. ROOSEVELT WROTE (AND PUBLISHED) SIX BOOKS BE-TWEEN 1887 AND 1889, A TIME WHEN HE WAS STAYING OUT OF POLITICS.

For three years after he lost the mayoral election, TR dabbled in a number of activities. He remained in New York attending to his duties as trustee of the Orthopaedic Hospital, director of the New York Infant Asylum, and assignments with several other institutions with which he was associated. He also continued writing.

Between 1887 and 1889, TR published six books. TR remained open to opportunities should they come along—which they did.

Even when he returned to politics, TR was always working on a book manuscript. TR wrote more books and magazine articles in his sixty years than some people can read in a longer lifetime.

In his preface to the third edition of *The Naval War of 1812*, TR chastised presidents Thomas Jefferson and his successor James Madison for their lack of preparation for war. (The fact that the book was printed in a third edition lent credence to the historical value of his work to readers.)

He stated, "It was criminal folly for Jefferson, and his follower Madison, to neglect to give us a force either of regulars or of well trained volunteers during the twelve years they had in which to prepare for the struggle that any one might see was inevitable."

Again, he could not see into the future, but he faced some of the same monetary restraints as Jefferson and Madison did almost 100 years prior to his presidency.

All in all, TR's first book was a success. It did not make him rich, but it helped him build a reputation as a scholar and military tactician, two talents he developed more fully as he took on more and more responsibility in his many political positions. It certainly encouraged him to accelerate his writing career, especially in the publication of books.

Topics ranged from biography (*Thomas Hart Benton*) to history (*Hero Tales from American History*), which he co-authored with Henry Cabot Lodge, his future conspirator in the charter fiasco; nature (*The Deer Family*, with T.S. Van Dyke, D.G. Elliot, and A.J. Stone); and politics (*American Problems* and *The New Nationalism*). The latter two appeared in 1910, along with his *Presidential Addresses and State Papers, 8 Volumes*, shortly after he left the presidency. If nothing else, readers had a clear history of TR's years as U.S. president and a keen insight into what was wrong with America.

Teddy Trivia

There was a three-year gap between the publication of *The Naval War of 1812* and his next book, *Hunting Trips of a Ranchman, Parts 1 and 2*. After that, he produced books almost every year, regardless of what his job happened to be at the time.

Fact #43. President Harrison appointed Roosevelt to the Civil Service Commission in 1889, because of Roosevelt's known reformer tendencies.

Losing the mayor's race did not hurt TR. It opened more doors for him. After the election, people in high places began to see his potential and appointed him to positions on the local and national levels that helped him refine his leadership skills. The experiences in the years between the mayoral race in 1886 and the gubernatorial campaign of 1898 provided the seasoning he needed to enter the toughest political arena of all: the presidency of the United States.

The Republicans nominated Benjamin Harrison as their presidential candidate in 1888. TR campaigned vigorously throughout the Midwest for the nominee. Harrison emerged victorious after a hard campaign. He did not forget TR's support.

One of the issues on which Harrison campaigned was civil service reform. He favored the merit system over the patronage system, but his was not a particularly popular position among members of Congress. He wanted someone on the United States Civil Service Commission who would not care particularly what Congress had to say about one side versus the other. He needed a reformer on the Commission, and Theodore Roosevelt was the perfect candidate.

On May 7, 1889, President Harrison appointed TR to the United States Civil Service Commission, along with another reformer, Hugh Smith Thompson, the former governor of South Carolina and assistant secretary of the treasury under Harrison's predecessor, Grover Cleveland. Much to the surprise of the *New York Times*, TR accepted the nomination.

A reporter wrote in the May 7, 1885, edition of the *New York Times*, "It was at first feared that he would not accept the position, as it requires a residence in Washington for a great deal of the time." The rest of the reporter's statement provided an insight into the psyche of Theodore Roosevelt, suggesting that he needed some publicity in his work, even if he had to relocate to get it.

Teddy Trivia

The United States Civil Service Commission was created on January 16, 1883, as part of the Pendleton Civil Service Reform Act to oversee the federal government's civil service. The law required some applicants to take civil service exams to get designated jobs and prohibited elected officials and political appointees from firing or removing civil servants in some situations.

FACT #44. ROOSEVELT WAS INSTRUMENTAL IN STOPPING VOTE-BUYING CORRUPTION, WHICH ENDED UP CAUSING HIS PATRON, PRESIDENT HARRISON, TO LOSE THE NEXT ELECTION.

TR retained his post with the Commission for the next six years. He took his duties seriously—so seriously, in fact, that he drew a lot of criticism and unwanted attention for doing a job that many people in government did not take seriously. As usual, he developed unique ways of handling his critics.

TR did an end run to convince congressmen who opposed him to comply with his reforms. He simply got the public involved. He explained:

> Occasionally we would bring to terms these Senators or Congressmen who fought the Commission by the simple expedient of not holding examinations in their districts. This always brought frantic appeals from their constituents, and we would explain that unfortunately the appropriations had been cut, so that we could not hold examinations in every district, and that obviously we could not neglect the districts of those Congressmen who believed in the reform and therefore in the examinations.

Those congressmen usually came around to agreeing with TR as he continued his reform efforts.

President Harrison was aware of TR's dislike of political patronage and partisan influence. The new commissioner sank his teeth into the job immediately with his usual zeal for rooting out spoils wherever he saw them.

TR had experience in the civil service reform arena. He had served as a member of the New York Civil Service Reform Association in the early 1880s. As a New York state assemblyman, he worked to pass the first state civil service act in the nation, the New York State Civil Service Act of 1883. He worked just as hard on the national level to create a civil service system that would attract the best people into government.

As commissioner, TR espoused three major principles: The civil service system should create equal opportunities for all citizens, not just those who knew certain politicians; the only people who should be appointed to federal jobs were those who had the right experience; and public servants should not suffer for their political beliefs or gender. (One of his accomplishments in his six years in office was opening civil service positions to women.)

If those principles were met, fraud and political abuse in government would be wiped out, and corrupt government officials would be exposed. The system worked just fine.

TR's reach was far and wide as he strove to implement fairness in the civil service system. He did not tolerate violations of his principles or of the code. Only one week into the job he recommended that examination board members in New York be fired for selling test questions to the public for $50.

And, to show that he did not play favorites regardless of who appointed him, he ordered Baltimore police to arrest postal employees who were buying votes for the re-election of President Harrison. The practice did not help President Harrison. In a game of presidential Ping-Pong, he lost the 1892 election to Grover Cleveland, whom he had defeated in 1888. Even though Cleveland was a Democrat, he reappointed TR to the commissioner post.

Teddy Trivia

TR acknowledged that he made enemies as Civil Service commissioner. He said, "I have made the Commission a living force, and in consequence the outcry among the spoilsmen has become furious. But I answered militantly that as long as I was responsible, the law should be enforced up to the handle everywhere, fearlessly and honestly."

FACT #45. THE PULLMAN STRIKE OF 1894—AND THE GOVERNMENT'S USE OF FORCE TO END IT—MADE ROOSEVELT WONDER IF HE WOULD BE BETTER OFF SPENDING HIS EFFORTS ELSEWHERE.

There were a couple of incidents in TR's second term as commissioner that made him step back and wonder if he could be doing more elsewhere to fight corruption. Even though there were tangible signs that he was effecting change, he wasn't sure he was doing enough. As he saw it, labor was still driving the economy, and workers were still on the short end of the stick.

When two of the largest employers in the United States, the Philadelphia and Reading Railroad and the National Cordage Company, failed in 1893, it set off a nationwide depression. The stock market tumbled;

banks and investment firms called in loans; companies fell into bankruptcy; and unemployment rates reached 25 percent. More than 15,000 companies closed their doors during the crisis.

The deep recession of 1893 affected TR adversely. So did the Pullman Palace Car Company strike of 1894. The ongoing depression of 1893 forced the company to reduce its workforce by 75 percent, rehire some workers, and then cut wages. Through all this, the company refused to lower the rent for workers who lived in company-built houses. Eventually the workers went on strike.

The Pullman strike was the first national strike in U.S. history. For the first time, people were exposed to unsatisfactory labor issues and a hint of socialism because of Eugene Debs's union leadership. TR and other reformers saw an opportunity in the strike to balance the economic differences between labor and capitalism. But another problem surfaced: excessive force by the U.S. government to quell the strike.

Courts invoked the Sherman Act against labor unions, instead of against the company. President Cleveland dispatched federal troops to Chicago to suppress the strikers. Those actions forced TR to step back and analyze the need for balance.

TR realized "that an even greater fight must be waged to improve economic conditions, and to secure social and industrial justice, justice as between individuals and justice as between classes." And, he "began to see that political effort was largely valuable as it found expression and resulted in such social and industrial betterment."

Later, as president, TR would use the Sherman Act in a way he found much fairer: He ordered the first antitrust suit under the Sherman Act. His aim was to dissolve Northern Securities Company, a holding company formed in 1901 by business financier J.P. Morgan and railroad entrepreneurs James J. Hill and Edward H. Harriman to dominate railroad traffic in the West. The company controlled the stock of the Great Northern, Northern Pacific, and the Chicago, Burlington and Quincy railroads.

Teddy Trivia

The principal author of the 1890 Sherman Anti-Trust Act, the first federal statute designed to limit the actions of cartels and monopolies, was U.S. Senator John Sherman (R-Ohio).

FACT #46. IN 1895, ROOSEVELT BECAME POLICE COMMISSIONER OF NEW YORK CITY.

TR's next chance to fight graft and corruption came in New York City, with its population of 2 million people. Recently elected Republican Mayor William Strong offered him the opportunity to serve as the head of the street-cleaning department. TR passed that up. He did not feel that he had the experience. But there was an opening on the Board of Police Commissioners, which the mayor offered as an alternative.

One of TR's oldest friends, Henry Cabot Lodge, pressed him to accept the position, which gave him the opportunity to return to his home base and root out corruption. On May 6, 1895, Mayor Strong appointed TR to the four-member board, at a salary of $5,000 per year. His appointment, which was for six years, lasted only two.

Strong appointed three other members: Frederick D. Grant, a Republican and oldest son of former President Ulysses S. Grant; Andrew D. Parker, a Democrat who would eventually become a thorn in TR's side; and John Monks, another Democrat. His co-commissioners elected him as board president. TR left Washington, D.C., that same day to fight City Hall—literally.

TR should have gotten an inkling of the problems besetting the Board of Police Commissioners right away. Two outgoing members, both Republicans, were asked to resign, but they refused. Therefore, the new mayor, a Republican, ousted them under the Power of Removal Act. Both former commissioners protested their removals vigorously—especially since a member of their own party sent them packing.

The biggest obstacle TR faced was the setup of the board. It was designed to make sure nothing could be done to influence the way the police department functioned. The board included two Democrats and two Republicans. That almost assured that the members would not agree on much.

TR promised to be nonpartisan as police commissioner. He wrote, "I was appointed with the distinct understanding that I was to administer the Police Department with entire disregard of partisan politics, and only from the standpoint of a good citizen interested in promoting the welfare of all good citizens."

The commissioners appointed a police chief who they could not remove without a trial subject to review by a court. The chief and a single commissioner could stop anything proposed by the other three commissioners. That had the potential to create permanent deadlocks among the commissioners.

To compound matters, the mayor appointed the commissioners, but he could not remove them unless the governor of New York agreed. That was not likely in most cases due to the machinations of Tammany Hall, the political machine that ran the city and the state. Tammany Hall seemed to be exceeding its own levels of greed and graft where the department was concerned.

Finally, the commissioners could appoint police officers, but they could not fire them without a trial and a subsequent review by the courts. That was a political structure that almost guaranteed that any attempts at reforms would be difficult at best, if not outright impossible. Some men might have thrown up their hands in despair. TR did not.

Fact #47. During his term on the board of commissioners, Roosevelt befriended the muckraking journalist Jacob Riis.

TR began a long friendship with Riis when he was a young man, but it evolved to a higher level when he started his police commissioner stint in New York City. The two men conducted night police patrols of the city together.

In December 1889, *Scribner's Magazine* published Riis's photo essay of New York City slum life. The next year an expanded version came out in book form, titled *How the Other Half Lives*. TR read the book and took action once he became the police commissioner by ordering the police to close the lodging houses they ran—where Riis had often resided in his youth.

Riis provided an invaluable service for TR. He had grown up in the slums of New York City, where he had lived in boarding houses run by the police department for poor people, which TR closed during his regime as commissioner.

Riis knew the slums of the city backward and forward and took TR to places he might never have found on his own. The visits gave TR fresh insights into the depressed conditions in which some New York City residents lived and prompted him to make some major changes to improve their lives.

Jacob Riis revealed in his biography of TR that New York City Police Chief Byrnes warned the new commissioner that police work would break him. "You will yield. You are but human," Byrnes said. Riis reported that it did no such thing. TR's answer "was to close the gate of the politicians to police patronage," which was his plan all along.

The first time TR and Riis went on patrol together, they discovered that 90 percent of the patrolmen assigned to duty were nowhere to be found. Riis commented on that in the newspaper the next day. His story had the desired effect.

Starting the next day, and throughout TR's term as police commissioner, more cops started taking their jobs seriously—and patrolling their beats lest he should find them missing.

As a result of their working arrangement, Riis and TR formed a mutual admiration society. Riis, in summing up TR's work as police commissioner, wrote, "We rarely realize, in these latter days, how much of our ability to fight for good government, and our hope of winning the fight, is due to the campaign of honesty waged by Theodore Roosevelt in Mulberry Street [the Police Department's headquarters]."

Riis rated high among TR's friends and influences. TR credited Riis with opening his eyes wider to the problems of tenement living and the need to resolve them.

Years after TR left the White House, he said that his "whole life was influenced by my long association with Jacob Riis, whom I am tempted to call the best American I ever knew." That was the level of esteem TR held for Riis the reformer—and for Riis the friend.

Fact #48. Roosevelt's insistence on enforcing the prohibition against drinking alcohol on Sundays led to anti-Roosevelt feelings.

TR walked into chaos his first day on the job in the form of a piece of legislation designed to reform the police department and render him practically useless. That was the Ainsworth Bill, sponsored in the New York

State Assembly by Danforth E. Ainsworth in his final year as an assemblyman.

Among its provisions, the bill changed the title of chief of police to superintendent of police and increased the incumbent's power. It also gave the superintendent the authority to try all cases of charges against members of the force. And, the bill stipulated that the superintendent could be removed from office only if he was deemed to be totally incapable of running the department. In effect, the superintendent would be untouchable.

Not surprisingly, the incumbent chief of police, Thomas F. Byrnes, supported the bill completely. The commissioners did not. They found an ally. Mayor Strong vetoed the bill, which did not pass. That spelled doom for Chief Byrnes.

According to a lengthy May 28, 1895, article in the *New York Times*, Chief Byrnes retired at his own request after thirty-two years of service. He was granted a $3,000 per year pension. Inspector Peter Conlin was named to replace him. The reporter noted that Byrnes's retirement "effectually disposes of the statement which had gained circulation that charges were to have been preferred against the retiring chief."

Two days after Chief Byrnes's departure, Acting Chief Conlin laid down the law to his administrators. He said: "The captains and acting captains were warned that there must be no laxity in the enforcement of [the excise laws] on Sundays and during the prohibited hours," and that "courteous, polite treatment of citizens would be insisted upon."

That same day, the board accepted the retirement of several other officers, except for one captain "against whom charges had been filed."

TR had been on the job only three weeks and he had already made it clear that reforms had started.

TR took aim at the street patrolmen as well as administrators. He was the epitome of an equal opportunity enforcer of laws and police procedures. One of his goals was to emulate his Civil Service Commission days and make merit rather than patronage the system for hiring and promoting police officers. One attempt in particular got him into trouble with city residents and caused him to wonder if he really wanted to be the police commissioner.

New York City had a law against drinking on Sundays, which the police conveniently overlooked. He decided to enforce it, mainly because he believed laws had to be obeyed, even if he considered them unfair or impractical. That created a stir in the city.

Residents were forced to find outlets at places like Coney Island to grab a beer. German-Americans in particular were incensed that their beer gardens were closed on Sundays. They held an anti-Roosevelt parade. Some people went so far as to mail bombs to TR. Fortunately, they were defused.

Fact #49. As police commissioner, Roosevelt instituted an innovative hiring process.

Commissioner Roosevelt could not get used to the constant resistance he received to even the best-intentioned moves to upgrade the police department. One of his fellow commissioners in particular, Andrew Parker, began opposing him on issue after issue. A feud developed between the two men that became counterproductive. The resistance perplexed TR. TR wrote:

> [We were] right in excluding politics from promotions . . . It was because of our acting in this manner, resolutely warring on dishonesty . . . and refusing to pay heed to any consideration except the good of the service and the city, and the merits of the men themselves, that we drew down upon our heads the bitter and malignant animosity of the bread-and-butter spoils politicians.

TR did some positive things to boost the morale of the police force and improve officers' efficiency. The board made it a point to reward officers for exemplary performance. "During our two years' service we found it necessary over a hundred times to single out men for special mention because of some feat of heroism," he wrote.

TR was aware that the merit approach was not perfect. He stated that competitive examinations were a means to an end. They did not always mean that the people who passed them would turn out to be ideal public servants. But, he explained, the examination system was better than the patronage alternative.

He cited as an example the appointment of 2,000 new police officers in New York City at one time when he was the police commissioner. There were 6,000 to 8,000 candidates for the openings. The commissioners had two choices in selecting the successful applicants: rely on outsiders' recommendations or apply the competitive examination. He preferred the examination route, which the board chose.

Under TR's leadership, all the applicants underwent rigid physical and mental examinations. Those who passed took the written competitive examination, which was not particularly rigorous. As TR described the test, it required "only the knowledge that any good primary common school education would meet—that is, a test of ordinary intelligence and simple mental training."

As he said, the tests were not foolproof. Sometimes potentially good recruits failed and men who turned out to be bad cops passed. Generally, he said, "As a rule, the men with intelligence sufficient to enable them to answer the questions were of a type very distinctly above that of those who failed."

In any event, the new competitive examination system marked an innovative step forward in the New York City police department's hiring process—and a success for TR.

The list of accomplishments was impressive, but it was not all TR wanted to get done. Despite his good intentions, the job wore him down. He was ready for a new, less taxing job. President William McKinley came to his rescue and appointed him assistant secretary of the navy. It was back to Washington, D.C., for the Roosevelt family.

Teddy Trivia

In his brief tenure as commissioner, TR and his fellow commissioners introduced a bicycle squad and pistol shooting practice, standardized officers' use of pistols, installed telephones in station houses, implemented annual physical exams for officers, and instituted new disciplinary rules. They appointed 1,600 new recruits based on their physical and mental qualifications, rather than on their political affiliations.

Part 5

The War Years

FACT #50. IN 1897, PRESIDENT MCKINLEY NAMED ROOSEVELT AS ASSISTANT SECRETARY OF THE NAVY AS WAR WITH SPAIN LOOMED.

President McKinley had taken notice of TR's performance as the commissioner of police in New York City. He needed a man with TR's energy and efficiency to run the civilian wing of the U.S. Navy, which was in need of an upgrade, particularly since a war with Spain loomed on the horizon. The primary issue between the United States and Spain in the 1890s was the overbearing conduct of the Spanish governor in Cuba. The United States was also worried that Spain was exerting too much power in the Caribbean, contrary to the Monroe Doctrine. Cuban revolutionaries' activities against the Spanish were increasing. The instability and political unrest in the region rattled U.S. authorities.

Some of TR's most reliable friends, most notably Henry Cabot Lodge, urged the president to appoint the brash young man as assistant secretary of the navy. He heeded their advice.

On April 19, 1897, President McKinley named TR to the position. TR may have been an assistant technically, but he turned himself into the de facto commander of the navy and gave Washington, D.C., a taste of what was to come when he became president. That was something no one envisioned at the time.

TR assumed his naval duties at a time when the organization was in a state of disarray and war with Spain was on the horizon. The navy was woefully unprepared for a war. President McKinley knew that. He did not want the United States to get involved in it unless there was no diplomatic way to avoid it. In that, he and TR disagreed. His new assistant secretary of the navy began at once to prepare the service for the war he was sure could not be averted and which a lot of people did not want.

In his autobiography, TR noted that he was in the minority at the time in preparing for the war. He said that "The big financiers and the men generally who were susceptible to touch on the money nerve, and who cared nothing for National honor if it conflicted even temporarily with business prosperity, were against the war." So were philanthropists, newspapers, and most of the Congress.

"Most of the Congressmen were content to follow the worst of all possible courses, that is, to pass resolutions which made war more likely, and yet to decline to take measures which would enable us to meet the war if it did come," TR proclaimed. He planned to proceed with his preparation, despite the opposition he faced. And he did it as if he were running the show.

Teddy Trivia

The title of assistant secretary of the navy was created in 1861, during the Civil War. The incumbent's job was to oversee the navy's civilian personnel and administer its shore facilities. The government did away with the position in 1869 after the war ended but reinstated it in 1890. It was discontinued for good in 1954.

FACT #51. ROOSEVELT ORDERED THE PRODUCTION OF "COAST DEFENSE BATTLESHIPS" TO PREPARE FOR THE WAR—AND TO GET AROUND THOSE WHO FELT THE NAVY SHOULD ONLY BE USED TO DEFEND THE COAST.

Many of the navy's ships were unseaworthy, and it was lacking in auxiliary vessels to support the large warships. Worse, the public was not in favor of building new ships. The navy resorted to subterfuge to tell citizens what it was building.

Traditionally, most Americans, including political leaders, believed their navy should operate solely to protect commerce and the U.S. coast. They did not believe big warships were needed to do that. TR disagreed. He believed that a large navy with powerful warships was essential to fight wars and keep the peace. TR insisted that he abhorred war. But, he said, "I advocate preparation for war in order to avert war; and I should never advocate war unless it were the only alternative to dishonor." Nevertheless, he did in the case of the Spanish-American War.

TR pushed for large, technologically advanced battleships—even if they had to be called something else. For a while, to get around the label "battleships," the navy started calling its new warships "armored cruisers." Then it switched the terminology to satisfy the people who believed only in the "coast and commerce" role for the navy.

The new ships became "coast defense battleships." The ships that fell into that category lacked seaworthiness and coal capacity. So the navy started building bigger and better ships labeled "sea-going coast defense battleships."

At the start of the Spanish-American War, the navy had on its active list six battleships, two armored cruisers, thirteen protected cruisers, six steel monitors, eight old iron monitors, thirty-three unprotected cruisers and gunboats, six torpedo boats, and twelve tugs. There were no auxiliary vessels other than the tugs to support them. In other words, the navy entered the Spanish-American War with a motley collection of warships that TR alleged could not win a battle. He vowed to change that.

One of the first things TR did in his first year was what he did best: identify the right people with whom to work. He socialized and communicated with naval historian Alfred Thayer Mahan and naval strategists Commodore George Dewey and Captain Robley D. Evans, and developed plans for fighting what he considered an inevitable war with Spain. Then, he appointed Dewey to command the Asiatic Squadron. The latter accomplishment was just the type of move that drove some of TR's critics—and supporters—to distraction.

Even though he was the "assistant secretary," TR had a penchant for setting policy on his own initiative, especially when the secretary of the navy, John Davis Long, was out of office, which was often. Long had a penchant for taking extended lunches, breaks, and vacations to his native New England for long periods to escape the hot Washington, D.C., summer weather.

Additionally, Long was not interested in the mundane day-to-day details of navy administration. He left those to TR, which he later regretted. TR did try to keep Long apprised of what he was doing. He wrote detailed letters to the secretary to update him on his activities, but Long mostly ignored them at his own risk.

Teddy Trivia

Alfred Thayer Mahan began his U.S. Navy career as an officer in the American Civil War. He believed naval power was the key to strong foreign policy, which he stressed in his 1890 book, *The Influence of Sea Power upon History, 1660–1783*. The book, which TR reviewed for the *Atlantic Monthly* in 1890, influenced the navy as it strengthened its forces and developed new strategies.

FACT #52. ROOSEVELT'S PENCHANT FOR DIRECT ACTION LED HIM TO APPOINT PEOPLE TO POSITIONS WHEN HE DIDN'T ACTUALLY HAVE THE AUTHORITY TO DO SO.

TR's talent for identifying and appointing the right people for the right purpose came to the fore in the Spanish-American War. Where he could not appoint people directly, he influenced the people who could. It was due largely to his influence that Admiral George Dewey, the commander at the decisive Battle of Manila, which started the war, received his position, although there were officers senior to him. It was TR who ordered Dewey to sail for Manila in the Philippines to take up a position to fight the Spanish navy. He sent the order when his boss, John Davis Long, the secretary of the navy, was out of the office!

Ten days after the *Maine* sank, Long took a day off to relieve the stress of being on a war footing. He told TR emphatically not to do anything that would impact the navy—or the country. That was like telling him not to attack graft wherever he encountered it.

TR began at once to move ships, people, ammunition, and materiel into place for the war he was sure was about to begin. In effect, he promoted himself to acting, rather than assistant, secretary of the navy.

He sent a cablegram to Dewey on February 25, 1898, with specific instructions:

> *Dewey, Hong Kong: Order the squadron, except the Monocacy, to Hong Kong. Keep full of coal. In the event of declaration of war Spain, your duty will be to see that the Spanish squadron does not leave the Asiatic coast, and then offensive operations in Philippine Islands. Keep Olympia until further orders.—ROOSEVELT.*

TR knew that *Monocacy* was unfit for war or anything else. The thirty-two-year-old ship had been built during the Civil War. It was emblematic of the mixed collection of "something old, something new, something borrowed" fleet the navy maintained. And the *Olympia* had been ordered to return to the United States. Based on TR's orders, it stayed in the Pacific and led the U.S. armada in the Battle of Manila Bay.

Long was not pleased with Roosevelt, which was nothing new. He considered TR a "bull in a china shop." But he seldom did anything to stop his assistant's rash behavior. According to the papers Long wrote after he left office, despite occasional differences of opinion, the conservative small-navy secretary got on well with the impetuous large-navy assistant and was sorry to see him go off to war in 1898. Off he went, though, as a lieutenant colonel in the United States Army.

Long may not have known what TR was up to a large part of the time, but the newspapers did. The *New York Sun* said in an article that "the liveliest spot in Washington . . . is the Navy Department. The decks are cleared for action. Acting Secretary Roosevelt . . . has the whole Navy bordering on a war footing. It remains only to sand down the decks and pipe to quarters to action."

Teddy Trivia

John Davis Long was born in Maine in 1838. He served as a congressman from Massachusetts and the state's governor before becoming Secretary of the Navy in 1897. Long is credited with laying the groundwork for the "new navy" developed under President Theodore Roosevelt—Long's former assistant, who actually did a lot of the work.

FACT #53. WANTING TO BE ACTIVELY INVOLVED IN THE WAR, ROOSEVELT JUMPED SHIP FROM THE NAVY (WHERE HE WAS A CIVILIAN) AND JOINED THE ARMY.

Even though TR had put a lot of time and effort into preparing the navy for war, he could not participate with it since he was not a member. He was itching to get involved actively in the fighting. On May 10, 1898, he resigned from the navy and "joined" the army, even though he had no military experience to speak of.

TR had a serious desire to test his mettle in war—any war. He believed that young men—and he considered himself one of them, even though he was forty years old at the time—should always be prepared to serve their country as a way to prove their strength and courage. He gave himself the opportunity to follow his own advice.

At the onset of the Spanish-American War, the army was in worse shape than the navy. It did not have enough troops to conduct a skirmish, let alone a war. Consequently, President McKinley called for 125,000 volunteers to supplement the army. More than a million men responded—including TR, as a recruiter and a soldier.

One of TR's considerable strengths was his ability to organize. That asset came to the fore as he and his old friend Leonard Wood raised a regiment of volunteer cavalry called the "Rough Riders." Their official name was the First U.S. Volunteer Cavalry.

The regiment consisted of a unique group of rugged Westerners, most of them from the southwest territories of the United States. TR became their leader. "Colonel" Roosevelt went off to war. Long wondered if his former assistant had lost his sanity.

Long gave credit where credit was due. In his journal, he admitted that TR "has been of great use; a man of unbounded energy and force, and thoroughly honest, which is the main thing." But, he opined, "He has lost his head in this unutterable folly of deserting the post where he is of most service and running off to ride a horse and, probably, brush mosquitoes from his neck on the Florida sands."

TR pulled a few strings to get his commission. One of his champions was Secretary of War Russell A. Alger. Alger, a Civil War veteran, was fond of TR and a patient of Leonard Wood. He offered TR command of one of the National Volunteer Cavalry regiments being raised. Later, Alger would try to block TR's Medal of Honor recommendation.

In that last statement, he was wrong. TR went a lot farther than Florida, geographically and accomplishment wise.

The secretary also provided insight into TR's character. "His heart is right, and he means well, but it is one of those cases of aberration—desertion—vain glory; of which he is utterly unaware. He thinks he is following his highest ideal, whereas, in fact, as without exception, he is acting like a fool."

The most significant comment Long included was a prediction that came true. "And yet," he wrote, "how absurd all this will sound if, by some turn of fortune, he should accomplish some great thing and strike a very high mark." TR did "accomplish some great thing," but that did not diminish the acumen Long displayed in his remarks.

Teddy Trivia

According to TR, "The young men of the country should realize that it is the duty of every one of them to prepare himself so that in time of need he may speedily become an efficient soldier—a duty now generally forgotten, but which should be recognized as one of the vitally essential parts of every man's training."

FACT #54. ROOSEVELT WAS THE ONLY ONE OF HIS ROUGH RIDERS WHO HAD A HORSE WHEN THE REGIMENT REACHED CUBA.

Roosevelt was in charge of a group of approximately 1,000 Rough Riders, of whom he knew little, since he had not personally recruited them. He suspected that they were good horsemen because most of them came from the Southwest. As he wrote about them later, "In all the world there could be no better material for soldiers than that afforded by these grim hunters of the mountains, these wild rough riders of the plains."

Beyond the fact that they were sturdy men, TR did not know much of anything about their training, when—or if—they would be called to action, or how the army planned to utilize them. He learned that the army did not have a clue, either.

TR's problem was not recruiting men. He wrote, "Within a day or two after it was announced that we were to raise the regiment, we were literally deluged with applications from every quarter of the Union. Without the slightest trouble, so far as men went, we could have raised a brigade or even a division. The difficulty lay in arming, equipping, mounting, and disciplining the men we selected."

TR recalled that while he was still assistant secretary of the navy he had tried to find out what the Department of War's strategy for fighting the war was. He said tersely, "They had no plans. Even during the final months before the outbreak of hostilities very little was done in the way of efficient preparation." Nevertheless, he and Wood began training their troops.

The Rough Riders were a diverse group. The 1,000 members were ranchers, cowboys, gamblers, and a few outlaws. The Easterners in the unit were primarily college dropouts and young men from the "upper crust" of society who were looking for a little adventure in their lives. They shared one basic asset: All of them were ready to fight.

A training camp was set up at San Antonio, Texas, to equip and prepare their unit for combat. They did so knowing that their chances of getting into battle were slim. Even though the army had attracted large numbers of recruits, not all of the units to which they were assigned were fit for battle. The Rough Riders had an advantage: Wood was an experienced war-fighter and a Medal of Honor recipient. That medal added a bit of luster to the Rough Riders's reputation.

By the end of May 1898 the Rough Riders were as ready for battle as they were ever going to be. They shipped off to Tampa, Florida, and left from there for Santiago de Cuba on June 13, minus a critical element of their cavalry equipment: their horses.

The War Department was in such haste to get troops to Cuba that it did not pay enough attention to the logistical side of the operation. The only way the horses could have gotten to Cuba was by swimming. So the Rough Riders arrived in the battle zone without their horses, which reduced them from a cavalry unit to an infantry regiment. That did not matter once they got into combat, as long as their leader had a mount.

TR was the only Rough Rider who had a horse when the unit reached Cuba. But he did not have a dress uniform, which he did not need for combat purposes anyway. He had only his service uniform—the only uniform he had in his short stint in the army.

Teddy Trivia

The Rough Riders may have been better off without their horses. Their steeds were not heavy enough for cavalry use, and many were unbroken. Half the horses bucked when riders mounted them or, according to TR, "possessed some other of the amiable weaknesses incident to horse life on the great ranches." Some of the animals were unmanageable, even for Rough Riders.

FACT #55. UNDER ROOSEVELT'S LEADERSHIP THE ROUGH RIDERS HELPED WIN THE BATTLE OF SAN JUAN HILL.

Once the Rough Riders arrived in Cuba, they joined the Fifth Corps, a well-trained and well-equipped unit comprised of a combination of volunteers and regular army soldiers. It was not long before they were pressed into battle at Las Guasimas, a village not too far from Santiago. That was a prelude to the Battle of San Juan Hill.

The battle at Las Guasimas exposed a weakness in TR's unit. The men were not used to walking or to the hot, sultry Cuban weather. As a result, only 500 Rough Riders participated in the fighting.

TR remained cool under hostile fire. He was finally getting the chance to test his mettle in a war, one that he had agitated for so vociferously. He was not entirely sure of what he should do at times as the fighting raged.

The American forces sustained several casualties at the Battle of Las Guasimas. Eight Rough Riders were killed; thirty-four were wounded. Altogether, of the 964 American soldiers in the battle, sixteen were killed and fifty-two were wounded.

At first the strategy of the American forces at the Battle of San Juan Hill was to drive their Spanish opposition off the high ground by firing at them from fairly static positions along a line below the hills. TR saw the folly in that and advocated a charge up the hills.

He ordered the Rough Riders to attack. Other troops joined them. The battle intensified as they rushed up toward the enemy positions.

TR led the charge on his horse, Little Texas. Since he was the only man there on horseback, he reached the crest of Kettle Hill before the infantry soldiers. There, he nearly ran into a wire fence, at which point he dismounted and parted with Little Texas. He did not expect to see his horse again—or anything else. A couple of bullets had scraped Little Texas, and one had grazed TR in the elbow.

The charge up the hill had turned into a contest among members of the Rough Riders and other units to see who could reach the top first. The issue was never truly settled. What mattered was who won the battle. That was indisputably the Americans.

The chaos of battle continued. TR noted, "It is astonishing what a limited area of vision and experience one has in the hurly-burly of a battle." At one point he led a charge on Spanish positions only to learn that he was virtually alone. His men had not heard his order. He returned to his troops, chided them for not following, reissued his order, and led the charge once again.

TR was no longer commanding only Rough Riders as the fighting continued. During the confusion of battle, unit integrity faded. Members of individual units broke up and merged with one another. TR was leading an amalgamation of troops; all followed him in pursuit of the Spanish troops.

Gradually, the fighting ended and the Americans won a significant victory at the San Juan hills. Once again, they paid a steep price for their effort. The Rough Riders regiment employed 490 men at the Battle of San Juan Hill. Eighty-nine were killed or wounded. That was the highest number suffered by any U.S. cavalry regiment engaged in the battle. The fighting was more intense than it had been at Las Guasimas, which resulted in the Rough Riders's high casualty count.

FACT #56. AFTER THE BATTLE, ROOSEVELT WAS NOMINATED FOR A MEDAL OF HONOR—BUT IT WASN'T BESTOWED FOR ANOTHER 103 YEARS.

Two controversies arose after the Battle of San Juan Hill ended. One involved returning the Rough Riders to the United States immediately. The other was a Medal of Honor recommendation for Roosevelt.

On August 3, 1898, the commander of the U.S. troops in Cuba, Major General William R. Shafter, held a meeting with the medical and commanding officers of the Fifth Corps at Santiago. Shafter read a letter from Secretary of War Alger ordering him to move the troops to the interior of Cuba. The order ran contrary to the officers' wishes. They wanted their troops returned to the United States to alleviate the risk of tropical diseases such as malaria and yellow fever.

TR expressed his concerns to General Shafter in a letter explaining why the troops should be sent home. In the letter, TR wrote, "I write only because I cannot see our men, who have fought so bravely and who have endured extreme hardship and danger so uncomplainingly, go to destruction without striving so far as lies in me to avert a doom as fearful as it is unnecessary and undeserved."

Shafter handed the letter to a correspondent for the Associated Press. The resulting publicity upset Secretary Alger and may have played a role in the subsequent denial of TR's Medal of Honor recommendation. Once the troops returned to the United States, action on approving the Medal of Honor languished—for the next 103 years.

Even though Alger had a soft spot in his heart for TR, he was not keen on authorizing the Medal of Honor for the Colonel. The bad publicity that resulted from the news in the press discouraged him and President McKinley from pursuing the matter.

After McKinley was assassinated in September 1901, TR took over as president. He did not feel that it was right for him to authorize his own Medal of Honor. (Alger had been dismissed for incompetence by that time.) After TR left office in 1909, the matter remained in limbo.

After Congress eliminated the statute of limitations on Medal of Honor awards, Roosevelt family members, congressional representatives, and other supporters pressed for the authorization of TR's award. The army continued to resist their pleas.

Some army historians felt that he had not really earned the medal. They argued that other soldiers had done as many brave things at the Battle of San Juan Hill as the Colonel had, and they were equally deserving of Medals of Honor.

Eventually, due to pressure from TR's supporters, the army relented. In a White House ceremony on January 16, 2001, President Bill Clinton presented TR's Medal of Honor to Tweed Roosevelt, TR's great-grandson. The award was a long time coming, but it was welcome to the Roosevelt family.

The award of the Medal of Honor to TR closed a memorable chapter in his life. He returned to the United States with a trace of malaria, a lot of bittersweet memories, and renewed ambition to pursue his political career. His successes in previous government positions and the acclamations he received for his service in Cuba opened new possibilities for him—in New York.

Teddy Trivia

Until 1996, there was a statute of limitations for awarding a Medal of Honor. The recommendation had to be submitted within two years of the action. The subsequent review process could take eighteen to twenty-four months. In 1996, Congress repealed the statute of limitations on military decorations. That cleared the way for a reexamination of TR's award.

Part 6

From Governor to President

FACT #57. ROOSEVELT BRILLIANTLY MANIPULATED THE REPUBLICAN PARTY INTO NOMINATING HIM FOR GOVERNOR OF NEW YORK IN 1898.

After earning the public's respect for his exploits in Cuba, TR looked for new fields to conquer. The next logical step from a political standpoint was the governorship of his home state of New York.

New York state politics were rough-and-tumble in the late nineteenth century. The state government was rife with corruption, and political bosses ruled the roost. Some of those bosses were less than happy when they learned that TR was contemplating a run for governor. He had been anti-machine and anti-corruption as an assemblyman. There was no reason for them to believe that he would be any different as governor. Their fears that he would attempt radical reforms were justified.

TR was a bit of an enigma from a party standpoint in New York. The Democrats ruled the political landscape for the most part in New York City and at the state government level. TR, as a Republican, was pretty much an interloper. Even his own party members did not always trust him completely, since he was not their model of a "machine" Republican. After all, he showed anti-business tendencies at times and even worked with Democrats on occasion for what he perceived as the common good.

When the gubernatorial campaign began in 1898, neither party knew what to expect from TR. He gave them an idea in the way he wrangled the Republican nomination.

The Republicans believed that TR intended to attack corruption in their party if he won the governor's office. The Democrats were sure that he was going to launch a statewide anti-corruption campaign against both parties. Republicans were a bit reluctant to nominate him, then.

TR took advantage of a new political group, the Citizens Union, to ensure Republican support. He approached Citizens Union leaders and suggested that they form a ticket to run against both major parties. The group's executive committee thought that was a swell idea and assumed that TR was going to head the ticket. He didn't do anything to dissuade them from the notion.

The committee launched a petition campaign to get the party on the ballot and collected 6,000 signatures. Naturally, the signers believed TR was heading the ticket. So did the Republicans, who feared that the new party might have a chance to win the election with TR as their candidate.

That created a quandary for them, since the incumbent governor, Frank S. Black, was a Republican. But his administration had been plagued by corruption and scandals. Their solution was simple. Dump Black and nominate Roosevelt.

TR ran his campaign in a low-key fashion, based more on his popularity than any specific platform. He promised the voters he would run a "clean" administration without outlining anything specific. That was enough for them, although his election was far from a landslide.

In the gubernatorial election of 1898, TR attracted 661,707 votes. His Democratic foe, Augustus Van Wyck, had 643,921. The Citizens

Union nominee, Theodore Bacon, received 2,103 votes. New York State had a new governor: Theodore Roosevelt. His tenure was short-lived, however.

Teddy Trivia

In his autobiography, TR understates the end run he did around the party bosses to secure the nomination: "In September, 1898, the First Volunteer Cavalry, in company with most of the Fifth Army Corps, was disbanded, and a few days later, I was nominated for Governor of New York by the Republican party." Those words disguised the political chicanery to which he resorted to get the party's nod—and at which he was adept.

FACT #58. AS GOVERNOR, THEODORE ROOSEVELT CREATED THE PALISADES INTERSTATE PARK TO CONSERVE THE HISTORIC LANDSCAPE.

As governor, TR worked closely with prominent New Yorkers and New Jerseyites to create the Palisades Interstate Park (PIP) to conserve a significant historic and national landscape. He urged the legislature, among other things, to push forest conservation, outlaw the use of feathers as adornments, and set aside land for public use. TR learned from the creation of the PIP that when government officials and members of the public worked together they could accomplish significant milestones in the area of conservation despite heavy opposition. He also learned more about the power of women.

In the late 1890s, large companies were destroying the Palisades Cliffs along the New Jersey side of the Hudson River to acquire gravel for roadbeds and broken stone for concrete. The quarries were not only eyesores but were creating irreparable damage to the environment. People living across the river in New York were upset about the destruction, too. Folks sought ways to stop the quarrying activities before the Palisades fell into the river.

The American Scenic and Historic Preservation Society, incorporated in 1895, was one of the leading opponents of the quarrying in the Palisades. The group was composed of many prominent socialites in the New York area who were determined to stop the destruction and save the Palisades and the Hudson River. TR knew many of them, since he traveled in the same social circles.

Clubs, newspapers, lawmakers, and other individuals and organizations joined the battle against the quarrying companies. They tried everything they could think of to shut them down. They even tried to get the army to establish a military base along the cliffs. The army was not interested. The businesses were too strong and withstood the lobbying—until women's suffrage stepped in.

Palisades quarries employed hundreds of workers. They shipped the stone as far away as New Orleans for $1 a ton. Workers blasted the stone, crushed it, loaded it onto barges, and shipped it. Not using expensive overland transportation made possible huge profits. It is no wonder the quarries did not want to close without a fight.

Astute politicians such as TR could see the handwriting on the wall. He had always promoted women's suffrage. The Palisades situation gave him a chance to work with them to accomplish something meaningful.

Members of the Englewood (New Jersey) Women's Club accepted the responsibility for ending the quarrying. They banded together with similar women's groups across the state to save the Palisades. They generated enough pressure and negative public opinion to attract the attention of lawmakers in New Jersey and New York.

Finally, in 1900, TR and his counterpart in New Jersey, Governor Foster Voorhees, signed legislation that made possible the solution to the problem. The Interstate Commission bought out the quarries and the Palisades were saved. The efforts enhanced TR's reputation as a conservation-minded politician, which he used as leverage when he reached the White House. That was where he truly stood out as a conservationist.

FACT #59. ROOSEVELT WAS THE ONE WHO ENCOURAGED JOHN MUIR TO START THE SIERRA CLUB.

Just as TR formed a series of friendships throughout his life that were durable and mutually rewarding, he also participated in some that were temporary and expedient. The latter category was important to him because of what he learned from each friend and how the knowledge shaped his life, regardless of how long the friendships lasted.

Among the people who entered his circle of friendship at critical times in his life and faded away as time went by and circumstances changed were people ranged from former presidents to the cowboys he fought with in Cuba. Regardless of who they were, they all shared a common bond: They helped shape TR's life—and vice versa.

John Muir, a noted conservationist, was one of these friends.

The credit for founding the Sierra Club goes to TR. He suggested to John Muir that such an organization would be a great asset for conservationists. Accordingly, Muir organized the club in 1892. He was its first president, and he served in that capacity until his death in 1914.

TR visited with John Muir in California in 1903 to discuss adding Yosemite Valley and the Mariposa sequoia grove to Yosemite National Park. He did not always agree with Muir, but expanding Yosemite National Park seemed like a good idea, so TR made it happen.

After Muir died, TR wrote a glowing tribute to him in the January 16, 1915, edition of *Outlook* magazine. He said:

> *Muir talked even better than he wrote. His greatest influence was always upon those who were brought into personal contact with him. But he wrote well, and while his books have not the peculiar charm that a very, very few other writers on similar subjects have had, they will nevertheless last long. Our generation owes much to John Muir.*

In retrospect, the same could be said about TR. By the time TR left the White House, conservation was a significant issue among politicians and the public. He happily reported those signs in his conservation initiatives as proponents became more active in their efforts.

After a 1901 hunting trip to Colorado, he wrote in *Outdoor Pastimes of an American Hunter*:

> *This high country is the summer home of the Colorado elk, now woefully diminished in numbers, and of the Colorado blacktail deer, which are still very plentiful, but which, unless better protected, will follow the elk in the next few decades. I am happy to say that there are now signs to show that the State is waking up to the need of protecting both elk and deer; the few remaining mountain sheep in Colorado are so successfully protected that they are said to be increasing in numbers.*

That single paragraph summed up his conservation concerns: diminishing numbers, the need for better protection, people's awakenings regarding the need for protecting natural resources, and successful results. It was a tribute to his conservation efforts as well.

FACT #60. AS EXPECTED (AND FEARED BY HIS POLITICAL OPPONENTS), ROOSEVELT WAS COMMITTED TO ROOTING OUT CORRUPTION IN NEW YORK—STARTING WITH THE CANAL SYSTEM.

TR assumed office on January 1, 1899. He quickly justified the Republicans' and Democrats' fears that he would attempt reforms, this time statewide instead of only in New York City. Governor Roosevelt pushed for—and got passed—some progressive legislation.

One of the most scandal-ridden departments in his predecessor's administration had been the state canal system office, where there was a need for a new administrator. The entire canal system was in danger of collapsing in 1898 due to insufficient funds. Work stopped suddenly on the partially completed "Nine Million Dollar Improvement," as it was called. The new governor would not allow that to happen.

From March 1898 to October 1898, it cost the state $450,000 to operate its canals, compared to $590,000 for the same period the previous year, a savings of about 25 percent. The comparative costs are somewhat misleading, since there was more activity on the canals in the 1898 fiscal year. That was TR's goal as governor: higher productivity for less cost.

Canal restoration was one of several issues TR addressed in his first year in office. He supported laws to advance civil service reform law in New York and the United States, improve conditions in tenement sweatshops in New York City, strengthen factory inspection procedures, limit work hours for public employees and women and children to eight hours a day, improve the public education system, and conserve resources.

He advocated a minimum wage for New York City schoolteachers, sought legislation to allow the state Supreme Court to inspect corporations' books, and backed anti-monopoly laws. One effort in particular incensed Platt and the party leaders: TR pushed through a new tax on public franchises. In the process, he was biting the hand that fed his political colleagues.

Large corporations in New York provided Republican Party leaders with hefty monetary donations. TR wasn't averse to political contributions; he was concerned that many of the corporations that provided the funding were not paying their fair shares of taxes.

TR was puzzled about why people opposed the franchise tax. He wrote, "I came to the conclusion that it was a matter of plain decency and honesty that these companies should pay a tax on their franchises, inasmuch as they did nothing that could be considered as service rendered the public in lieu of a tax." That settled the matter in his mind.

Many of the corporations that supported the party financially operated public franchises that supplied services such as water and gas. These franchises were not taxed. Neither they nor the political bosses wanted them to be. The governor did. He forced a franchise tax through the state legislature.

TR's justification for the franchise tax was clear. He said, "A change should never be shirked on the ground of its being radical, when the abuse has become flagrant and no other remedy appears possible. This was the case with the taxation of local franchises in this State." He won the argument.

Teddy Trivia

Equal taxation was a cornerstone of TR's governorship. He noted in his first annual message, "Absolute equality, absolute justice in matters of taxation will probably never be realized; but we can approximate it much more closely than at present." His attempts to achieve equality and justice in taxation created a rift with Republican Party leaders.

Fact #61. Roosevelt's opponents wanted him out as governor and his supporters wanted him to run for president, so the two groups formed a faction to get him elected as vice president.

TR angered the party bosses by doing what he did best: root out corruption. The new governor was not content to simply oversee the passage of laws. He enlisted the aid of the press corps to make sure the citizens of the state knew that he was working incessantly on their behalf and defying the machine. He knew the value of good public relations and newspapers.

TR also gained favor with the public as he traveled tirelessly around the state making speeches and presiding over ceremonial affairs. The people did not care much what he had to say. They were just happy that their governor made it clear he was on their side and that he was pursuing their interests despite opposition from legislators and party bosses. As a result, legislators and bosses alike grew somewhat reluctant to challenge TR.

While party leaders and TR agreed on some issues (such as conservation), they disagreed on others. They began to wonder if they wanted him in office for a second term. They sensed a power struggle looming between themselves and TR that favored him.

TR continued to govern, despite opposition from his own party leaders in many areas of his administration. That set up a conflict between the party bosses that spilled over into the entire Republican Party as different factions sought to find the right position for TR.

Some of TR's opponents wanted to bury him in a job where he could not harm them. His supporters wanted just the opposite; they sought a position that would give him some exposure to the voting public as a steppingstone to the presidency. After a great deal of infighting, the two factions arrived at a compromise: the vice presidency of the United States.

The perfect opportunity for the Republicans to move TR up—and out—of the state came quickly. U.S. President William McKinley was almost a lock for re-election in 1900. He had done well in his first term, and there was no reason to believe that he would not continue to retain his effectiveness. But he did not have a vice president as the election approached. Vice President Garret Hobart died of heart failure on November 21, 1899, and the party did not replace him. Roosevelt's name was placed into the mix. The idea captivated most high-ranking Republicans—including President McKinley.

Roosevelt raised strenuous objections to becoming vice president, claiming that he could not afford to pay his expenses in Washington, D.C., and that his supporters in New York State wanted him to remain as governor. Both arguments had merit.

The national clamor for him to be McKinley's running mate won the day, however. He threw himself into the campaign.

On March 4, 1901, TR became the vice president of the United States. He did not hold the position long.

Teddy Trivia

One of the things that kept TR going in New York was his ability to take a punch and keep on fighting. He said, "I no more expected special consideration in politics than I would have expected it in the boxing ring. I wished to act squarely to others, and I wished to be able to show that I could hold my own as against others." He proved as governor that he could do both.

Fact #62. On March 4, 1901, Roosevelt became vice president. Six months later, President McKinley was assassinated and Roosevelt became president.

Even though TR got caught up in a political fight not of his own choosing at the 1900 Republican Convention, he benefited ultimately from the outcome. He had some doubts about his duties as vice president for the few months he was in office.

TR did not exactly set the Senate on fire with his March 4, 1901, inaugural speech. It was short at only 411 words. And it was tepid. He closed by saying, "But there is also every reason for facing [these duties] with highhearted resolution and eager and confident faith in our capacity to do them aright . . . Most deeply do I appreciate the privilege of my position; for high, indeed, is the honor of presiding over the American Senate at the outset of the twentieth century."

His words outweighed his actions in the coming months. One problem TR faced as vice president was his inability to shape and implement his own policies. He had to follow the party line, which had never been his preference. And his duties were limited. His primary role was to preside over the Senate, which did not enthrall him. Regardless, he threw himself into the role even though he found it boring at best.

The fact that he had a limited knowledge of parliamentary procedures did not help him carry out his role—or impress the senators over whom he was presiding. Somehow, as TR always did, he muddled through until the Senate adjourned.

During the summer of 1901, TR returned to his retreat at Oyster Bay. He accepted speaking engagements and focused on foreign affairs. TR stuck to topics with which he was familiar: building the navy and alerting his audiences to the growing power of certain nations such as Germany and Japan. He and President McKinley were in agreement on many of TR's ideas, but they did not work together to develop them.

TR also began developing a base of support for a possible presidential campaign in 1904. The Republican nomination would be open, since McKinley would have completed two terms already. And TR realized that the popularity he had enjoyed after the Spanish-American War was fading, so 1904 might represent his best chance for running for president.

As TR laid the groundwork for his presidential campaign and honed his foreign relations expertise and skills, fate stepped in. An assassin named Leon Czolgosz shot President McKinley on September 6, 1901. McKinley died several days later, in the early morning of September 14.

TR took the oath of office the same day President McKinley died. In his typical courageous manner, he did not give a second thought to the danger that the position involved.

The twenty-sixth president of the United States, Theodore Roosevelt, told Congress in his first annual message on December 3, 1901:

> *No man will ever be restrained from becoming President by any fear as to his personal safety. If the risk to the President's life became great, it would mean that the office would more and more come to be filled by men of a spirit which would make them resolute and merciless in dealing with every friend of disorder.*

TR proved to be as resolute as the man he described in his speech. The continuity in the office of the president of the United States stayed in place uninterrupted as Theodore Roosevelt stepped into the White House.

Fact #63. Passing the Newlands Reclamation Act was Roosevelt's first priority when he assumed office.

One of the lessons TR had learned during his time in the Dakota Territory was that the western part of the United States was never going to grow if it did not have adequate water. That had been made abundantly clear by John Wesley Powell when he began exploring the West shortly after the Civil War ended. He noted that after the winter snow melted and the spring rains ended, the region went into a dry period. That was an impediment to farming, ranching, and increasing the population.

Powell suggested that an extensive irrigation system was needed to provide the badly needed water, and he mapped locations for dams and irrigation projects. A lot of people agreed with him, especially after a series of droughts hit the West in the 1890s. But nobody acted to do anything about the situation until TR stepped in.

Natural resources were not the focal point of the federal government at the turn of the twentieth century. Every project suggested was tied up in legalistic red tape. President Roosevelt was not a great fan of bureaucracy, so he looked for ways to do an end run around the people in charge of natural resources.

TR actively participated in drafting the reclamation bill to control what went into it and to prevent opponents from wrecking it by insisting on individual states' rights over national interests. In the process, he signaled lawmakers and the rest of America that he was a "hands-on" president, and that he would become involved personally in issues near and dear to his heart.

TR's first step was to tell Congress how vital the irrigation issue was in national interests. He did that in his first message to Congress on December 3, 1901. That same day several Western senators and congressmen formed a committee to draft a reclamation bill. The chief architect was Francis G. Newlands of Nevada, after whom the eventual bill was named.

It did not take long for Congress to pass a bill. On June 17, 1902, Congress passed "An Act Appropriating the receipts from the sale and disposal of public lands in certain States and Territories to the construction of irrigation works for the reclamation of arid lands." (The official name explains why the bill became known as the Newlands Reclamation Act.)

The act set aside the proceeds of the disposal of public lands for the purpose of reclaiming waste areas of the West through irrigation and building new homes upon the land. The settlers were responsible for repaying the money the government appropriated for the projects.

The repayments could be reused as a revolving fund that was available continuously for any work done. Work began immediately.

Without the Newlands Act and the water it made available, much of the West could not have been settled. Only ten months into his presidency, TR had accomplished a major piece of legislation that had significant repercussions for the entire country, not just localized sections. That was a major departure from ordinary federal government operations.

Five years after the initial passage of the act, the secretary of the interior created the United States Reclamation Service within the United States Geological Survey to administer the program. That same year, the service was renamed the United States Bureau of Reclamation.

Teddy Trivia

Twenty-eight irrigation projects attributed to the Newlands Act began between 1902 and 1906. They involved more than 3 million acres and more than 30,000 farms. Many of the dams built were higher than any constructed previously across the globe. The dams fed main-line canals over 7,000 miles in total length and involved the construction of tens of thousands of culverts and bridges.

FACT #64. DURING HIS FIRST TERM AS PRESIDENT, EDITH BOUGHT A HOUSE FOR HIM AS A RETREAT—WITHOUT TELLING HIM SHE WAS GOING TO DO SO.

During TR's first full term as president, Edith decided they should have a place away from the White House where he could unwind. She envisioned a rustic cabin where they could indulge in the types of outdoor activities they both liked. Edith was not sure he would go along with her, so she purchased a place in Virginia without telling him. It was about as rural as she could get.

Edith bought a fifteen-acre plot about a four-hour train ride and a ten-mile horseback or carriage ride away from Washington, D.C., (about 60 miles) with a small, fairly new cottage on it, on which construction began in 1903. She paid $280 for the "retreat," including alterations she made.

At the time of purchase, there was 12 feet by 32 feet of space on each of two floors. There were no stove, chimney, well, or toilet facilities, inside or out. Quickly, Edith had a ground floor partition removed, end fireplaces added, and the central stair moved to the side to create a single lodge room.

She named the place Pine Knot, since it was rife with pine trees. One month after she bought the place, Edith sprung her surprise on TR.

The president of the United States soon found himself at a retreat with no plumbing, no running water, and no electricity. They had to go to a spring down the hill from the cabin to fetch water. But, they had plenty of nature to keep them occupied. That was uppermost in Edith's mind when she bought the place.

A pretty wife, a successful hunt, and a cherished son to write to were the ingredients for a happy life for TR, especially in light of the many crises he was juggling simultaneously at the White House. Based on his letters about Pine Knot, it was a great place for him to get away, if only for a few days.

Edith may not have gotten her money's worth after all was said and done, but she did achieve a sense of self-satisfaction. TR and Edith did use Pine Knot, although not often. They visited the place at least nine times, mostly around Thanksgiving and Christmas, between 1905 and May 1908, their final "mini-vacation" there.

Sometimes the children would accompany them, but more often than not it was just Edith and TR alone with nature and each other, which suited both of them just fine. Among the children, only Alice never visited the retreat.

The Roosevelts never made any major improvements to the retreat. In July 1911, Edith Roosevelt purchased seventy-five more acres at Pine Knot, anticipating that her husband would run for a second full term as president. The family held on to the property until 1941, when Edith sold it to George Omohundro, their longtime neighbor and TR's hunting partner. That closed another chapter in the Roosevelt family's life, another one that held fond memories for them.

FACT #65. ROOSEVELT WAS THE FIRST PRESIDENT TO RIDE IN AN AUTOMOBILE IN PUBLIC—AND TO OWN ONE.

It was not often that anyone could take Theodore Roosevelt for a ride. But on August 22, 1902, he rode in a purple-lined Columbia Electric Victoria Phaeton during a parade in Hartford, Connecticut. Twenty carriages followed behind.

Normally, the carriage—or simply a horse—would have been TR's preferred mode of travel. And he always used a horse and carriage for official government purposes.

Cars were just becoming part of the U.S. government's travel fleet during TR's second term in office. In 1907, the Secret Service started using two White Company steamers it borrowed from the army to transport visitors to and from the railroad station in Oyster Bay, where TR spent time in the summer.

There was no official appropriation for the use of these cars, but he did use them occasionally. Consequently, he became the first president to ride (publicly) in a U.S. government automobile.

TR forecast correctly that automobiles would change the face of the country's future. He predicted that they would become more widely available to Americans, which would open access to the parks (TR always had nature and conservation on his mind!). He was right.

TR also owned a car, a Stanley Steamer. However much TR might have correctly predicted a future where people rode in cars rather than on horses, he was always a horseman through and through. From his childhood to his days in the Badlands to his leadership of the Rough Riders, horses were in his blood. An avid outdoorsman and hunter such as TR could hardly be otherwise. In his letters to his children, he recounts many stories of horseback riding, and describes the horses and what they were like, sometimes even down to the tack they were wearing.

In October 1903, he wrote to his son Kermit about the meeting of a horse and an automobile:

> *Yesterday afternoon Ethel on Wyoming, Mother on Yagenka and I on Renown had a long ride, the only incident being meeting a large red automobile, which much shook Renown's nerves, although he behaved far better than he has hitherto been doing about automobiles. In fact, he behaved so well that I leaned over and gave him a lump of sugar when he had passed the object of terror—the old boy eagerly turning his head around to get it. It was lovely out in the country, with the trees at their very best of the fall coloring. There are no red maples here, but the Virginia creepers and some of the dogwoods give the red, and the hickories, tulip trees and beeches a brilliant yellow, sometimes almost orange.*

Teddy Trivia

Technically, TR was not the first U.S. president to ride in an automobile. President McKinley rode in cars a couple times while in office, but never in public. Also, he was transported to a hospital in an electric ambulance after being shot. But TR holds the distinction of being the first U.S. president to ride in a car in public—and to own one as well.

FACT #66. ROOSEVELT CREATED THE FIRST BIRD RESERVATION.

Reclamation and forestry were two of TR's first priorities when he assumed the presidency. He had gained an appreciation for reclamation and conservation in his days in the Badlands and as the governor of New York. The White House gave him the influence he needed to push conservation on a national scale.

TR was a great supporter of the preservation of birds and took steps as president to make sure they were protected, something he had wanted to do since he was governor. In November 1899, TR wrote:

> *The State should not permit within its limits factories to make bird skins or bird feathers into articles of ornament or wearing apparel. Ordinary birds, and especially song birds, should be rigidly protected. Game birds should never be shot to a greater extent than will offset the natural rate of increase.*

TR believed that birds should be saved for utilitarian reasons, none of which had to do with money. He lamented the passage of birds like the passenger pigeon, which had been driven to extinction by habitat loss and overhunting. So he acted to make sure that they were protected. His efforts to do so were nothing new for him.

Ornithologists were concerned with the devastation hunters were causing among pelicans, herons, egrets, and other birds that featured commercially attractive plumage. They were beginning to reduce the numbers of those birds to the point that extinction was possible.

Many of the birds gathered at tiny Pelican Island, about four acres in size, located in the Indian River Lagoon on the east coast of central Florida. The ornithologists decided that was a good place to make a stand. Paul Kroegel, a local resident concerned with the pelicans on the island; the Florida Audubon Society; and the American Ornithologists' Union petitioned President Roosevelt directly for relief.

The president was all too glad to accede to the request. In typical fashion he did not want to waste time going through Congress or battling red tape. He asked his advisers if there was any law that would prevent him from declaring Pelican Island a federal bird reservation. None, they said.

Without fanfare, on March 14, 1903, he signed a proclamation stating simply, "It is hereby ordered that Pelican Island in Indian River in section nine, township thirty-one south, range thirty-nine east, State of Florida, be, and it is hereby reserved and set apart for the use of the Department of Agriculture as a preserve and breeding ground for native birds."

The first of the fifty-one bird refuges he created became a reality—and he did it without ruffling many feathers.

Teddy Trivia

When TR was governor of New York, making clothes and other articles of apparel with bird feathers was a common practice in the state. He expressed revulsion to the technique. As he emphasized, "Birds in the trees and on the beaches were much more beautiful than on women's hats." Since plume hunters were extremely busy in Florida, he decided to start his bird preservation activities there.

FACT #67. THE COAL STRIKE OF 1902 WAS ROOSEVELT'S FIRST MAJOR CRISIS IN OFFICE.

TR had been in office for about eight months when his first major crisis arose. Anthracite coal miners in eastern Pennsylvania went on strike in early May 1902 for higher wages and better working conditions. Normally, a local strike would not draw the attention of the president of the United States. This one was different.

Almost every American relied on coal for energy purposes at this point in history, and a lot of people panicked over the thought of disrupted supplies with winter approaching. The United Mine Workers, led by John Mitchell, and the owner of the mine, George Baer, who also owned the Philadelphia and Reading Railroad company, drew their lines in the sand. The scene was set for a battle involving TR.

Neither the union nor the mine owner budged as the strike began. Union leader John Mitchell took the initiative and asked the president to establish an independent arbitration committee to resolve the impasse.

TR asked his commissioner of labor, Carroll D. Wright, to look into the causes of the strike. Wright formulated a report that acknowledged each side's position and proposed reforms, including a recommended nine-hour workday on an experimental basis, instead of the standard ten-hour workday in place at the time, and limited collective bargaining.

TR held back Wright's report, lest he appear to be pro-union. And, even though Mitchell had proposed the committee, the miners refused to go along with arbitration. So did Baer. Eventually, TR set up a fact-finding group to study the issues and proposed his own solution.

Negotiations dragged on, and the president chafed to get fully involved. His attorney general, Philander Knox, cautioned him that he did not have the authority to intervene.

Lack of authority did not bother TR. Under pressure from the union, the owner, his own party, and the public, he threatened to replace the workers with army troops, by force if necessary. His goal was to mine coal, regardless of who was doing the work.

TR figured that the negotiators could work toward a settlement while the soldiers dug. The fact that they were not trained in the art of coal mining did not bother TR. His plan raised a few eyebrows among politicians, citizens, and everyone else who had a vested interest in settling the strike.

Secretary of War Elihu Root came to TR's rescue. He worked with banker J.P. Morgan, who had financial interests in Baer's railroad, to convince the miners that independent arbitration was in their best interests. Finally, they agreed. In mid-October 1902, President Roosevelt announced that an agreement to end the strike had been reached. The 163-day strike ended on October 23.

As a result of the solution to the strike, each side got a little of what they asked for. The miners received a 10 percent pay increase instead of the 20 percent they had demanded. Their workday was cut from ten to nine hours; they had asked for an eight-hour workday. They had also demanded recognition for their union by the mine owners.

The owners refused to recognize the UMW, but they were forced to accept a six-person arbitration board composed of equal numbers of labor and management representatives to settle subsequent labor disputes. As far as Mitchell was concerned, that was a de facto recognition of the UMW. The biggest winner, though, was TR. His popularity continued to grow, especially as he attacked the trusts that were so prominent in the country.

FACT #68. ROOSEVELT ORDERED THE FIRST ANTITRUST SUIT UNDER THE SHERMAN ACT.

TR had come down hard against big businesses when he was an alderman and governor, which was antithetical to traditional Republican Party policy. But, TR was not a typical Republican. He continued his "trustbusting" practices as president by urging Congress to control large corporations by whatever means possible.

TR felt that a first step regarding big business's influence in the United States was to convince the public that government should curb its power. Americans were leery of large trusts, but they were also skeptical of government regulation. He vowed to change public opinion about government's role in business and establish controls acceptable to citizens, business operators, and politicians.

TR did not want to eliminate big business's power completely; he wanted to mitigate it through practical regulation. The challenge required a balancing act. He started with a new Department of Commerce and Labor.

There were antitrust laws in place, most notably the Sherman Act of 1890, but TR did not think they had enough teeth and were not being enforced adequately. So in 1903 he convinced Congress that the country needed a department to oversee interstate commerce and labor relations.

In response, Congress created the Department of Commerce and Labor, the first new entity at that level the government had created since the Civil War. Businesses lobbied heavily against the creation, but they lost their battle. The department included a Bureau of Corporations, whose charge was to uncover violations of current antitrust laws.

Next, he ordered Attorney General Knox to start filing lawsuits against large monopolistic companies, including J.P. Morgan's Northern Securities Company, John D. Rockefeller's Standard Oil Trust, and James B. Duke's tobacco trust. Government attorneys launched the first of the forty-five such suits that were introduced during TR's administration. The fallout was almost immediate.

On February 19, 1902, TR ordered the first antitrust suit under the Sherman Act. He wanted to dissolve the Northern Securities Company. TR alleged that NSC was monopolizing railroad traffic between Chicago and the northwestern part of the country, which did not fit into his concept of fair business practices. When Knox filed the lawsuit on the basis of restraint of trade, Morgan and Republican Senator Mark Hanna from Ohio pleaded personally with TR to stop the lawsuit, but the president refused. Off to court they went.

NSC's attorneys argued that the company did not engage in interstate commerce; it was merely a stockholder. The case reached the U.S. Supreme Court. By a margin of 5–4, the justices agreed with the government and ordered the company's breakup. That was a major victory for the president.

The government's victory heightened TR's popularity with the people. More important, it put a halt to railroad operators' efforts to consolidate the nation's railroads into a monopoly and lessened business giants' zeal for creating holding companies.

Finally, it put the Morgans, Hills, and Harrimans of the business world on notice that they were not safe from anti-monopoly lawsuits or legislation. TR had already proved that to unions. Now he showed business owners that he was willing to regulate them as well.

Teddy Trivia

The NSC victory was only the first for TR. Later, other trusts, such as Standard Oil, suffered the same fate. President Roosevelt proved that he was an equal opportunity arbiter when it came to creating as stable a business environment as possible for U.S. companies.

FACT #69. ROOSEVELT WAS INSTRUMENTAL IN THE CREATION OF THE PANAMA CANAL.

By 1870, American trade with the rest of the world was expanding. That meant merchants would need more ships to transport their goods and shorter routes to accommodate them. The U.S. government turned to a project that had intrigued people for years: building a canal between the Atlantic and Pacific oceans.

Efforts to build the passage languished until 1899, when the U.S. Congress created an Isthmian Canal Commission to analyze the feasibility of a Central American canal and recommend a route.

Initially, the commission recommended a route through Nicaragua. Then it changed its decision. There the matter rested until a French company offered the United States its assets for $40 million. That revived American interest in the project. All it took was Theodore Roosevelt to get it going. First, though, he had some minor problems to resolve, such as turning Panama into a free country.

Panama joined Colombia in 1821 after a Central American revolt against Spain. Colombia posed a problem for TR during negotiations for rights to build the Panama Canal, since its government believed that he was bullying them into making a deal.

On January 22, 1903, TR's secretary of state John Hay signed the Hay-Herrán Treaty between the United States and Colombia. According to the terms, Colombia would grant a lease in perpetuity to the United States on a six-mile-wide strip across the Isthmus of Panama in exchange for $10 million and an annual payment of $250,000.

The U.S. Senate ratified the treaty on March 14, 1903, but the Colombian Senate did not follow suit. The Colombians held out for $25 million, which infuriated TR. He thought that was extortion. He looked for another way to gain access to the coveted canal ground.

The president believed that politically unstable Panama owed something to the United States, which had intervened in its internal affairs thirteen times between 1850 and 1900.

In the final fifty years of the nineteenth century, Panama had been ruled by forty administrations and suffered through fifty riots and five attempted secessions. When Panama declared its independence in 1903, the U.S. government supported it. That had as much to do with Colombia's intransigence in dealing with the Roosevelt administration over canal rights as it did with Panama's independence.

TR saw the Panama Canal as a necessary passage for expediting U.S. military forces around the globe. Consequently, he vowed to build the canal, which he said in his autobiography was the most important action he took during his presidency. Neither Colombia nor an effete U.S. Congress was going to get in his way.

President Roosevelt knew how to take advantage of an opportunity to accomplish something he wanted badly. News reached Washington that yet another revolution was beginning in Panama. The word was that the Panamanians would be happy to turn over canal rights to the United States under the same terms Colombia had rejected.

That gave TR an idea. After all, the United States had intervened in Panama's politics before. Why not now, when the United States had something valuable to gain?

The Panama Canal opened officially on August 15, 1914. It was a proud moment for the United States and Theodore Roosevelt, who, despite the controversy surrounding the project, saw it through to completion.

FACT #70. ROOSEVELT SUPPORTED PANAMA'S REVOLUTION—AND ENGENDERED A RAGING CONTROVERSY.

When Colombia balked at finalizing the deal to create the Panama Canal, TR saw an opportunity when the people of Panama began a revolution. After all, a Panamanian government might be easier to deal with than the Colombian government.

While he did not openly support the revolution in Panama, TR did let folks know through back channels that he would not oppose it. And, if a U.S. warship or two should show up in Panama by coincidence to support the rumored coup, so much the better. That is exactly what happened.

On November 2, 1903, the U.S. Navy's gunboat *Nashville* arrived in Colón, Panama, with a contingent of marines. That was "barely on time," according to TR. Another ten U.S. warships settled offshore. The day after *Nashville* arrived, the coup occurred. The coincidence was remarkable.

The Colombian troops there might have put down the coup, but they were reluctant to do so in the presence of the *Nashville*, the U.S. Marines, and the warships offshore that inhibited any attempts to reinforce them. Years later, TR claimed that the Colombian troops had actually supported the revolution.

Immediately after the coup ended, Panama declared its independence, which the United States and several Latin American countries recognized. Soon an agreement was reached.

The agreement allowed the United States to build a canal through a ten-mile-wide, perpetually leased section of central Panama, to use more land if needed, and to intervene militarily in Panama, which it had already done. It required the United States to guarantee Panama's independence and pay $10 million, plus $250,000 annually. Events moved quickly after that.

Panama ratified the treaty on December 4, 1903. The U.S. Senate did the same—or at least advised that it be ratified—on February 23, 1904. President Roosevelt signed it officially two days later.

The two countries exchanged ratifications on February 26, 1904, and proclaimed it official. That was record time for two governments to negotiate, draw up, and ratify a treaty of significant proportions. That was TR's intention from the get-go, and he could get things accomplished when he saw an opportunity.

TR was sure he had acted correctly. He wrote, "From the beginning to the end our course was . . . in absolute accord with the highest of standards of international morality. . . . To have acted otherwise . . . would have been on my part betrayal of the interests of the United States." Critics decried what he had done.

The *New York Times*, often a thorn in TR's side, proclaimed loudly that Roosevelt's coup was an "act of sordid conquest." Later, in a December 10, 1908, article, it admitted that "Roosevelt's Panama Canal Account Holds Up."

The Democrats had intimated that Roosevelt's deal with the Panamanians was a scheme to help his brother-in-law Douglas Robinson and President-elect William H. Taft's brother Charles make money.

Arguments over the affair continued long after the deal was completed. That was no surprise; TR's Panama Canal triumph may have been the most controversial action of his presidency. While the arguments raged, construction went on, with TR right there.

Teddy Trivia

TR noted in his autobiography, "A finer body of men has never been gathered by any nation than the men who have done the work of building the Panama Canal . . . they have all felt an eager pride in their work; and they have made not only America but the whole world their debtors by what they have accomplished."

Part 7

Roosevelt's Second Term

FACT #71. IN 1904, ROOSEVELT WAS ELECTED PRESIDENT ON HIS OWN MERITS.

TR was pleased with his accomplishments in his three years in office. So were the Republican Party and the American people. The party nominated him unanimously for a full term to continue what he had started. His platform was simple: maintain the protective tariff, increase foreign trade, uphold the gold standard, expand the merchant marine, promote a strong navy, and support the president's foreign and domestic policies.

The Democrats nominated Alton B. Parker, the chief judge of the New York Court of Appeals, who had served on the state's Supreme Court when Roosevelt was governor. He was not much competition. On November 8, 1904, TR was elected by a wide majority.

He was poised to continue his policies and presidential style for at least another four years. Once elected for his first full term, he jumped into it prepared to accomplish great things.

TR had a lot to be proud of after his first term. He had no intention of sitting on his laurels. He wanted to lead the United States into the twentieth century as a world power, knowing that all the turmoil across the globe would eventually involve the country. He also had ambitious plans for his domestic conservation and reform efforts. The president pursued his foreign and domestic agenda with a great deal of fervor and achieved notable results on both fronts.

In his inauguration speech on March 4, 1905, TR set the tone for his first full term in office. He told Americans that their country's international role was expanding out of necessity.

"We have become a great nation, forced by the fact of its greatness into relations with the other nations of the earth, and we must behave as beseems a people with such responsibilities," he said. "Much has been given us, and much will rightfully be expected from us."

TR stressed his usual message of "duties to others and duties to ourselves, and we can shirk neither." As events turned out, he took those words seriously.

TR also hinted at his domestic policy. He noted that industrial development had changed society tremendously, and not always for the better.

"The conditions which have told for our marvelous material well-being, which have developed to a very high degree our energy, self-reliance, and individual initiative, have also brought the care and anxiety inseparable from the accumulation of great wealth in industrial centers," he observed. His meaning was clear.

TR was going to address the "accumulation of great wealth" in the interests of righteousness and social justice. For him, the words he uttered were more than empty rhetoric. He intended to act. The ride began immediately.

FACT #72. WHEN ROOSEVELT VISITED PANAMA IN 1906, HE BECAME THE FIRST PRESIDENT TO VISIT A FOREIGN COUNTRY WHILE IN OFFICE.

TR was so excited about the Panama Canal project that he visited Panama in November 1906. That made him the first American president to visit a foreign country while in office.

His usual energy frustrated the Secret Service agents and trip arrangers. He made unscheduled visits to workers and hospitals and demanded to see places, people, and things that were not on the itinerary, such as work sites, black workers, military personnel, and steam shovels. By the time he left, people were glad to see him go so work could continue without his incessant interruptions.

As TR was aboard the U.S.S. *Louisiana*, heading home, he wrote to his son, Kermit:

> *Our visit to Panama was most successful as well as most interesting. We were there three days and we worked from morning till night. The second day I was up at a quarter to six and got to bed at a quarter of twelve, and I do not believe that in the intervening time, save when I was dressing, there were ten consecutive minutes when I was not busily at work in some shape or form. . . . When on Wednesday we approached the coast, and the jungle-covered mountains looked clearer and clearer until we could see the surf beating on the shores, while there was hardly a sign of human habitation, I kept thinking of the four centuries of wild and bloody romance, mixed with abject squalor*

and suffering, which had made up the history of the Isthmus until three years ago. . . . Then I thought of the rebellion against the Spanish dominion, and the uninterrupted and bloody wars that followed, the last occurring when I became President. . . . Now we have taken hold of the job [of building the canal]. We have difficulties with our own people, of course. I haven't a doubt that it will take a little longer and cost a little more than men now appreciate, but I believe that the work is being done with a very high degree both of efficiency and honesty; and I am immensely struck by the character of American employees who are engaged, not merely in superintending the work, but in doing all the jobs that need skill and intelligence. The steam shovels, the dirt trains, the machine shops, and the like, are all filled with American engineers, conductors, machinists, boiler-makers, carpenters. From the top to the bottom these men are so hardy, so efficient, so energetic, that it is a real pleasure to look at them. Stevens, the head engineer, is a big fellow, a man of daring and good sense, and burly power. All of these men are quite as formidable, and would, if it were necessary, do quite as much in battle as the crews of Drake and Morgan; but as it is, they are doing a work of infinitely more lasting consequence. Nothing whatever remains to show what Drake and Morgan did. They produced no real effect down here, but Stevens and his men are changing the face of the continent, are doing the greatest engineering feat of the ages, and the effect of their work will be felt while our civilization lasts.

FACT #73. THE SUPREME COURT UPHELD ROOSEVELT'S TRUST-BUSTING EFFORTS BY UNANIMOUSLY RULING AGAINST SWIFT & COMPANY.

The year 1905 got off to a favorable start for TR long before his Inauguration Day. The first piece of good news came on January 30, when the Supreme Court ruled unanimously for the United States in its "trustbusting" case against the meat packing firm of Swift & Company.

The Swift & Company decision affected interstate commerce and expanded federal power under the commerce clause of the U.S. Constitution by ruling that locally operated businesses that made products sold in interstate markets could be subject to federal regulation. The decision set a positive tone for the rest of the year—and his administration.

TR and reform were synonymous. He instituted reform in whatever political or appointed office he assumed, starting with his three terms as New York state assemblyman.

Readers of his autobiography will notice that the word "reform" appears in ten of the fifteen chapters. That fact highlights the importance TR placed on reform in every chapter of his life—and of the need for change in every aspect of American society.

Significantly, TR did not see reform as a one-party issue. He worked with Democrats and Republicans alike to implement reforms in every aspect of life for the benefit of society. His ability to work across party lines when it was expedient was one of his many talents and caused people to wonder at times whether he was truly a Republican or a Democrat.

In one case, TR worked closely in the New York State Assembly with a Democrat named Pete Kelly. He explained how that benefited both men: "We began to vote together and act together, and by the end of the session found that in all practical matters that were up for action we thought together. Indeed, each of us was beginning to change his theories, so that even in theory we were coming closer together."

TR carried his willingness to work with people of all political "isms" into every campaign and position. The fact that he formed his own political party in 1912 was evidence that he did not always agree with the Republicans with whom he was affiliated. And, he learned from Democrats as well as Republicans.

His ability to work across party lines manifested his willingness to learn and apply the lessons to the betterment of society—all society. His zeal for reform was an offshoot of his bipartisan nature. He worked well with people of different political beliefs whenever he found it necessary to do so. The civil reforms he enacted were—and still are—proof of that.

The civil reform changes TR initiated in New York State in the 1880s and continued in his tenure in Washington, D.C., set the tone for government merit programs across the country. They are still in place. That is one more tribute to his forward-thinking ways.

Teddy Trivia

The reforms TR started in New York State and across the country are still in place today. He was among the first politicians in the nation's history to see the connections among efficiency, individual character, merit, and corruption. His goal was simple: separate politics and corruption from individuals' opportunities to acquire government jobs based on merit, rather than political party affiliation.

FACT #74. ROOSEVELT ESTABLISHED THE NATIONAL FOREST SERVICE SHORTLY AFTER BEGINNING HIS SECOND TERM IN OFFICE.

Near the beginning of his second term, TR accomplished another milestone by establishing the National Forest Service. Four months later he made the Wichita Forest in Oklahoma the first federal game preserve. He established three more before his term ended: the Grand Canyon (1908); Fire Island, Alaska (1909); and National Bison Range, Montana (1909).

TR was not particularly active in pursuing conservation efforts in his first term as president. He appointed only one commission during those years, the Public Lands Commission. Its charge was to study public land policy and laws. He became more aggressive in his second term, much to Congress's chagrin.

For a while, world events such as seeking re-election, finding a solution to the Russo-Japanese War, and overseeing the building of the Panama Canal pushed conservation issues into a corner. But they were always foremost in his mind. When TR pushed conservation into the forefront, he did it with a vengeance.

Starting in 1907, TR appointed five more commissions. The first was the Inland Waterways Commission, which he appointed on March 14 to study the river systems of the United States, the development of water power, flood control, and land reclamation.

TR believed that the country's inland waterways had to be developed. The process involved many other important water problems, and he wanted them all considered before the development began. The Inland Waterways Commission began a flood of similar appointments. Before the flood began, TR issued a call to the governors of the nation's states and territories to gather in Washington, D.C., to determine what conservation issues had to be addressed. The crowd expanded beyond the governors. The attendees also included the members of the Supreme Court and the Cabinet and a collection of scientists and national leaders.

On June 8, 1908, he appointed the National Conservation Commission to prepare the first inventory of the natural resources of the United States. The commission was composed of four sections: water, forests, lands, and minerals. Each section had a chairman. Gifford Pinchot, who was the chairman of the executive committee, declared that the conference was the turning point in the conservation movement in American history.

Later in 1908, TR created the Country Life Commission. He appointed Liberty Hyde Bailey, director of the College of Agriculture at Cornell University in New York, as chairman. The commission's assignment was to study the status of rural life and make suggestions on how to integrate the lesser populated areas of the United States into mainstream America.

By that time, Congress was getting testy about TR's commissions. It refused to pay the printing costs for Bailey's final report, which advocated creating a large agricultural society in the United States. That did not impact the publication. The Spokane, Washington, Chamber of Commerce published the report.

The ramifications of the commission's work were far-reaching and long-lasting. The report provided by the National Conservation Commission encouraged TR to expand his conservation efforts. Even though the end of his presidency was nearing, he accelerated his attempts to push his agenda.

In the final analysis, TR accomplished quite a bit from a conservation standpoint in his seven years as president. One of his most significant contributions was in public relations. He raised the nation's awareness of the need for conservation and put "Big Business" on notice that it had to start paying attention to saving natural resources, even if he had to take them out of its hands—which he did.

Teddy Trivia

TR's conservation efforts included withdrawing coal, mineral, oil, phosphate, and water-power site lands from private exploitation. In the process, he relied on his old trick of enlisting allies who were best equipped to help him.

FACT #75. ROOSEVELT NEGOTIATED A SETTLEMENT BETWEEN JAPAN AND RUSSIA, AVERTING A POTENTIALLY CATASTROPHIC WAR BETWEEN THE COUNTRIES.

Russia and Japan went to war in February 1904 over the issue of who had dominance in Korea and Manchuria. The war was short, but costly, for both countries. By 1905, it was beginning to affect the rest of the world.

TR and his counterparts around the globe did not see any end in sight to the war, even though Japan was gaining the upper hand. They sought a way to stop the fighting before other countries became involved. TR stepped in to settle a dispute, as many people expected him to do. After all, he had settled the coal strike a couple of years earlier. Why not end a war as well?

In June 1905, TR volunteered to meet with delegates from the two countries to settle their differences aboard his presidential yacht, *Mayflower*, which was moored at Oyster Bay. Both sides agreed. He stayed there while the negotiators moved to the naval base at Portsmouth, New Hampshire, in August 1905 to hammer out the details of the peace talks.

Delegates shuttled back and forth between Portsmouth and Oyster Bay. It took a few weeks to negotiate a solution satisfactory to both sides, but Russia and Japan finally signed a peace treaty at Kittery, Maine, on September 5.

According to the terms, Russia recognized Japan as the dominant power in Korea and turned over its naval leases of Port Arthur, Manchuria, and the Liaotung Peninsula, as well as the southern half of Sakhalin

Island, to Japan. Both countries consented to restore power in Manchuria to China. The settlement was a political coup for President Roosevelt, but he had no illusions about its impact on peace around the world.

TR recognized that the growing power of Eastern countries and their opposition to interference from their Western counterparts was a powder keg waiting for a match. The fact that Japan had emerged victorious in a war against a traditional Western power—a first-time event for any Eastern country—was a signal to him, one that the United States needed to heed.

TR wrote in a September 8, 1905, letter to his political opponent and disarmament advocate, Carl Schurz, "Until people get it firmly fixed in their minds that peace is valuable chiefly as a means to righteousness, and that it can only be considered as an end when it also coincides with righteousness, we can do only a limited amount to advance its coming on this earth."

He did not believe peace was a viable option anywhere around the globe. The United States needed to flex its muscles in preparation. Before he could arrange for that, he received a pleasant reward for his efforts at Portsmouth.

Teddy Trivia

John Hay, TR's secretary of state, had been one of President Lincoln's secretaries. He and TR's father had also been friends. Even though TR wanted to conduct the Russo-Japanese War peace talks himself, it would have been too indelicate for him to remove Hay. Fate stepped in. Hay died in July 1905, which allowed the president to lead the negotiations.

FACT #76. ROOSEVELT CREATED THE IMMIGRATION RESTRICTION ACT OF 1907.

There was one unfinished piece of business for TR regarding Japan after he oversaw the Russo-Japanese War treaty. The Japanese had never been completely satisfied with the outcome of the negotiations. They were upset that he had blocked reparations they felt were due from the Russians.

The Japanese had another item that rankled them, which was not related to the treaty. They did not like the way Americans were treating their countrymen who had moved to the West Coast, specifically California. They believed that American farmers and laborers were mistreating Japanese immigrants.

In 1905, Japan annexed Korea, and its growing dominance in Manchuria—in defiance of China—continued. And the American public was becoming increasingly uncomfortable with Japan. By 1907, people in both countries felt that war might be imminent between Japan and the United States. TR sought to improve diplomatic relations between the two countries to avert it.

TR believed that Californians had a legitimate concern about Japanese immigration. He noted, "The people of California were right in insisting that the Japanese should not come thither in mass, that there should be no influx of laborers, of agricultural workers, or small tradesmen—in short, no mass settlement or immigration."

Immigration complaints and dissatisfaction over the terms of the Russo-Japanese treaty were Japanese concerns in TR's viewpoint. He had a secondary issue to consider: The United States had established bases in the Philippines, which were closer to Japan than to the United States. He wanted to protect those bases as the United States expanded its foothold in the Eastern Hemisphere, which would be difficult in the event of Japanese aggression. The president instructed Secretary of State Elihu Root to sit down with the Japanese to reach an accord.

There was a small breakthrough in 1907 when the two countries reached a "gentlemen's agreement" on immigration numbers. The Japanese agreed to limit the number of people coming to the United States, while the Americans promised to recognize the presence of the Japanese already living in the United States; to permit entry to their wives, children, and parents; and to avoid legal discrimination against Japanese children in California schools. That promise did not stop some Americans from discriminating against Japanese immigrants, however.

As a follow-up to the 1907 agreement, Root struck a deal with the Japanese ambassador to the United States, Kogoro Takahira, which really did not address the core issues. In the pact signed on November 3, 1908, the United States and Japan pledged to maintain the status quo in the Far East, recognize China's independence and territorial integrity, support an "open door" policy in China, and consult one another if further crises erupted in the Far East.

The mutual "hands-off" agreement was a temporary fix, but the clamor for and fear of war between the two countries abated after Root and Takahira arrived at their accord. Should it flare up again, TR was ready.

FACT #77. ROOSEVELT WAS THE FIRST OF ONLY FOUR PRESIDENTS TO WIN THE NOBEL PEACE PRIZE.

TR was always looking for ways to improve processes and save money for the citizens. He gave them a direct example of how to use money for the public good after he won the Nobel Peace Prize.

The Nobel Prize Committee singled out TR for his prowess in negotiating peace between Japan and Russia. On December 10, 1906, it awarded him the Nobel Peace Prize. It was the first time in its five-year history that the Nobel Prize had been awarded to an American. It was also the first half of the singular Nobel Prize and Medal of Honor combination awarded to TR, who became the only U.S. president to earn both.

TR tried to downplay the significance of the award, which included a large gold medal, a diploma in a fancy case, and a cash stipend. He was more interested in the intangible rewards: knowing that he had ended at least one war and the prestige that went along with the prize. He vowed to donate the money to various charities. TR advised the committee accordingly in his acceptance speech, which he did not deliver personally. That honor went to Herbert H. D. Peirce, who gave it in Oslo, Norway, on December 10, 1906.

Peirce, TR's third assistant secretary of state, had been responsible for arranging the deliberations of the Russo-Japanese War at Portsmouth, New Hampshire. He was also the first person outside the negotiating rooms there to learn that a settlement had been reached. Peirce was the U.S. minister to Norway from August 13, 1906, to May 30, 1911.

In his speech he said simply that if he had not been president of the United States, he would not have been involved in the peace process. Therefore, he advised the money truly belonged to the people of the United States.

TR, in his typical altruistic fashion, proposed to use it as seed money for a "foundation to forward the cause of industrial peace . . . of righteousness and justice, the only kind of peace worth having." The foundation was never established. Instead, he donated the money to World War I relief projects.

Ed Renehan, Jr. mentioned in his book, *The Lion's Pride*, that TR made twenty-eight war donations. He explained: "A few of the gifts included $6,900 to the Red Cross; $5,000 to Eleanor for her Y.M.C.A. project; an additional $4,000 to the YMCA National War Work Council; and $1,000 to Edith's sister, Emily Carow, a volunteer with the Italian Red Cross at Porto Maurizio, Italy."

TR was in no rush to pick up the money or the Nobel Prize. He waited until 1910, when he just happened to be in the area of Norway. He visited Christiana (renamed Oslo in 1925) to receive both. True to his word, TR turned the medal over to the White House, where it still resides.

FACT #78. ROOSEVELT WAS A FOUNDING MEMBER OF THE NATIONAL INSTITUTE OF ARTS AND LETTERS.

From the time he was at Harvard, TR was a great "joiner." His eclecticism qualified him for a variety of associations. Among them were the National Institute of Arts and Letters and the American Academy of Arts and Letters.

The American Academy of Arts and Letters, created in 1898, was called the National Institute of Arts, Science and Letters. By 1900, the "Science" part was dropped, and eventually the organization morphed into the American Academy of Arts and Letters. Name changes notwithstanding, TR was one of the first fifteen members.

The NIAL held its first meeting in February 1899 in New York City. It had a maximum membership of 150. The primary qualification for membership was the completion of notable achievements in art, music, or literature. TR qualified through his accomplishments in literature. Thus, he became an original member. In 1904, he was among the first fifteen NIAL members elected to the organization's AAAL offshoot.

Eventually, TR used some of his influence to try to get the group a federal charter. That created a bit of controversy. He relished the chance to get the institute and the academy more recognition. It was a bit of a surprise that his last controversy as president would arise from such an innocuous attempt to gain recognition for a literary organization.

In January 1909, as TR was leaving office, his friend, Senator Henry Cabot Lodge of Massachusetts, a historian in his own right, introduced a bill to incorporate the American Academy of Arts and Letters and the National Institute of Arts and Letters. The list of incorporators included Lodge, TR, and what the *New York Times* called in a January 18, 1909, article, "A Slur on the Immortals," "a galaxy of leading writers, scientists, sculptors and artists." The newspaper did not take the organizations as seriously as they took themselves.

The members of the Institute of Arts and Letters objected to being called "Immortals," because it made them sound like elite French academicians. They considered themselves to be nothing more than a group of artists pursuing practical policies for their mutual benefit as part of an official organization—preferably one with a federal charter.

According to Lodge, TR, et al., the incorporation would benefit the country. They included in their bill a provision that the government might call on members of either organization to get advice on literary matters when needed. A Judiciary Committee deleted the provision. Worse, it denied the "immortals" a charter, offering to incorporate the groups in Washington, D.C., to deprive them of national recognition. The slap in the face did not deter TR or Lodge.

Within a few days of the Judiciary Committee's ruling, TR issued an executive order to form a National Fine Arts Council and appoint an Advisory Arts Committee to the Government, which individuals involved claimed was independent of the attempts to incorporate the institute and the academy.

Coincidence or not, the organizations did not get their charters before TR left office. The National Institute of Arts and Letters was incorporated by Congress in 1913, one of the last papers signed by outgoing president, William H. Taft, TR's successor. The American Academy of Arts and Letters was incorporated in New York State in 1914 and received its federal charter in 1916.

In any case, TR was not affected. He had earned his way into both organizations, did what he could to help them while he was in office, and remained a member in good standing, since acceptance carried with it a lifetime membership.

Fact #79. Roosevelt sent the navy on a grand global tour between 1907 and 1909 to showcase America's military might.

One of the president's primary motivators for the American navy's 1907–1909 grand global tour was to let the Japanese know that the United States had modern, technologically advanced ships and that he could—and would—employ them anywhere in the world if necessary. That was the underlying reason for what would become known later on as the voyage of the "Great White Fleet."

As commander in chief of the armed forces, President Roosevelt was proud of "his" new navy, especially the battleships that had been added to the fleet—and which he had played a part in building. He wanted to let the rest of the world share in his pride and announce that the United States was strengthening its navy in anticipation of taking its foreign duties seriously.

TR knew that other nations were building bigger and better ships to protect their maritime resources around the globe. He had seen what the Japanese Navy had done in the Russo-Japanese War in 1905 and realized the potential of the British ship, H.M.S. *Dreadnought*, the first of the modern "all-big-gun" battleships, which had been launched in 1906. As modern as the "Great White Fleet" was to TR, it was in danger of becoming obsolete.

Navies were also experimenting with submarines, airplanes, and other modern weapons. The president felt that it was time for the United States to display its naval prowess. Despite opposition from several quarters, he dispatched a U.S. Navy fleet on a voyage around the world.

There was a great deal of ceremony as the ships left Hampton Roads, Virginia, on December 16, 1907, en route to their first stop, Port of Spain, Trinidad. TR watched from the yacht *Mayflower* as the fleet under the command of Rear Admiral Robley D. Evans, aboard the battleship *Connecticut*, sailed away. As impressive as the sight was, there was an undercurrent of deception involved in the undertaking. All was not as it seemed.

On the outside, the ships were gleaming. The interiors were a different matter. Some of the ships had malfunctioning engines. Two, *Alabama* and *Maine*, had to drop out along the route. They were replaced by *Wisconsin* and *Nebraska*; if any more had been unable to continue, there would have been no substitutes.

The navy sent every battleship it had on the cruise, except for two that were not seaworthy. Even the fleet commander had to be replaced when the fleet reached San Francisco. The ailing Admiral Evans turned command over to Rear Admiral Charles S. Sperry.

The fleet was composed of sixteen steel-clad, steam-powered battle-ships, all built after the Spanish-American War, and numerous auxiliary support vessels crewed by 14,000 sailors and marines. Destroyers and other ships dropped in and out along the way as the goodwill tour progressed, with a few diversions.

As the ships sailed into Hampton Roads on February 22, 1909, there was TR, aboard *Mayflower*, to greet them, just as he had seen them off.

It was one of his final acts as president. The fleet returned just three weeks before TR was scheduled to leave office.

When President Roosevelt sent the Great White Fleet on its world-wide tour, he had several goals in mind: He wanted to test the navy's readiness, promote international goodwill, and make sure the countries around the globe understood that the United States was a naval power. TR had stated before he dispatched the fleet that he wanted "all failures, blunders and shortcomings to be made apparent in time of peace and not in time of war." In that respect, the cruise was a success.

Teddy Trivia

The cruise was by no means uneventful for the sailors, especially in Brazil. A bar brawl erupted in Rio de Janeiro between sailors from the *Louisiana* and local longshoremen that threatened to create an international incident. But representatives from the navy and Brazil ironed out the misunderstanding and the fleet moved on.

FACT #80. ROOSEVELT FIRST USED THE TERM "BULLY PULPIT" TO DESCRIBE THE PRESIDENCY.

TR was an ardent conservationist. He collaborated with whatever individuals and organizations were willing to work to protect the nation's natural resources for their own and future generations. TR was especially active in his seven and a half years as president, during which he confronted opponents of conservation, such as business people and Congress, with steely resolve. He and his collaborators saved millions of acres and protected wildlife for the American people. His conservation legacy is still being felt today, and no doubt will be for generations to come.

TR told Congress in his seventh annual message on December 3, 1907, that "The conservation of our natural resources and their proper use constitute the fundamental problem which underlies almost every other problem of our national life." He had a perfect platform from which to deliver that message.

The White House provided the pulpit; he delivered the sermons. But he did more than sermonize. TR practiced what he preached. He began by coining the phrase "bully pulpit."

He said, "I suppose my critics will call that preaching, but I have got such a bully pulpit!" "Bully" had been one of his favorite words for years. He used it to describe something great. All he did was combine it with "pulpit" and a new phrase was born.

Conservation was not a new issue for TR when he assumed the presidency in 1901. He had been pushing it for years. As a child, TR had learned the need to treat animals with respect and maintain a balance of nature to conserve their numbers for the benefit of hunters and society. It was a natural extension of that belief to press for conservation of natural resources.

His egalitarian motives for conservation were evident in this passage from "Wilderness Reserves: The Yellowstone Park":

> *It is entirely in our power as a nation to preserve large tracts of wilderness, which are valueless for agricultural purposes and unfit for settlement, as playgrounds for rich and poor alike, and to preserve the game so that it shall continue to exist for the benefit of all lovers of nature, and to give reasonable opportunities for the exercise of the skill of the hunter, whether he is or is not a man of means.*

TR began his conservation efforts long before entering the White House, albeit in a limited fashion. As a member of the New York State Assembly, he was too involved in fighting graft and corruption to address conservation issues. But TR did donate a large part of his Roosevelt Museum of Natural History to the Smithsonian Institution.

TR learned early in life that hunters needed to be conservationists. After all, needlessly slaughtering animals was counterproductive to their hunting activities. TR saw the need for a code of ethics among hunters as a step to ensuring a steady supply of wildlife. As usual, when he saw a need for something, he acted.

FACT #81. ROOSEVELT MADE THE UNITED STATES A WORLD POWER.

The government and people of the United States spent their first 125 years trying to define their role in the world. For the most part they stayed out of international politics, with occasional forays into wars with the Barbary Pirates between 1801 and 1815, Mexico in 1846–1848, and Spain in 1898. It was not until TR became president that the United States began its ascendancy as a world power.

Years after TR left the White House, President Wilson was still talking about the navy in terms of defense. In his annual message to Congress on December 8, 1914, he said:

> *A powerful Navy we have always regarded as our proper and natural means of defense; and it has always been of defense that we have thought, never of aggression or of conquest. But who shall tell us now what sort of Navy to build? We shall take leave to be strong upon the seas, in the future as in the past; and there will be no thought of offense or provocation in that. Our ships are our natural bulwarks.*

Since TR's first day on the job as assistant secretary of the navy, he had pushed for a strong offensive navy. Historically, the U.S. Navy had been a defensive force. TR made it clear to anyone who would listen— and to some who would not—that the way to earn respect from other nations with strong armed forces was to create a powerful navy. And, he stressed, there should be shortcuts, such as a canal between major oceans, to make travel across the globe easier.

Until the aftermath of the Spanish-American War, the United States had never had any territory outside North America to administer. Once the federal government took responsibility for the Philippines, Guam, Puerto Rico, Cuba, and Hawaii after 1898, it had to play a bigger role in international politics to protect American interests in those jurisdictions. That was a major reason TR increased U.S. involvement in global affairs.

President McKinley had started the job of expanding the United States's international presence. TR took it a step further. He did not restrict his efforts to export American ideas and values to his years in the White House. TR continued to push for U.S. involvement in world affairs when it became evident to him that World War I would become a reality.

TR's insistence on letting the world know that the United States was willing to use diplomacy when necessary to keep peace among nations or military power to protect its interests led to a new role for the country. He was the first United States president to establish the country as a world power, and his persistence and statesmanship set a precedent that every one of his successors has followed, albeit reluctantly at times.

In the final analysis, TR was not just "any" president. He was the right person to be in office at the turn of the twentieth century, when the United States needed a "modern" president. Theodore Roosevelt fit that need, even though it took a human tragedy, the assassination of William McKinley, to get him into the White House. TR started the United States down the road to international relevance.

FACT #82. ROOSEVELT PROMISED NOT TO RUN FOR A THIRD TERM—AND KEPT THE PROMISE.

TR's role as U.S. president ended in 1909, but that was not the end of his political career. However, he made a promise that he would not run for a third term. True to his word, he honored that promise, but insisted on picking a nominee as his replacement.

"I regarded the custom [of not running for a third term] as applying practically . . . to a President who had been seven and a half years in office as to one who had been eight years in office . . . in the teeth of a practically unanimous demand . . . that I accept another nomination, and the reasonable certainty that the nomination would be ratified at the polls . . . the substance of the custom applied to me in 1908."

He persuaded the Republicans to nominate his secretary of war, William Howard Taft, for president. Taft won the election easily over his Democratic opponent, William Jennings Bryan. As of March 4, 1909, TR was out of the White House—but not out of politics. He did not rule out another term eventually, since he believed that "the third term tradition has no value whatever except as it applies to a third consecutive term."

TR proved the truth in that statement after he saw what happened to the United States once he left office. He eventually considered that third term.

As his presidency ended, TR cast about for new opportunities. He settled immediately on one that gave him a chance to remain in the public's eye and continue to espouse his views on matters he deemed important. TR accepted a position as contributing editor of *Outlook*, a leading journal of the time, with which he had a longstanding relationship.

TR's first article for *Outlook*, "The Higher Life of American Cities," was included in the December 1895 issue. His choice to work with *Outlook* was so important that the *New York Times* trumpeted it in a March 5, 1910, article, "Roosevelt Begins Work as an Editor."

TR's first eleven pieces as contributing editor for *Outlook*, which were published quickly in book form, demonstrated his eclecticism at its finest. Topics ranged from "A Scientific Expedition" to "Where We Cannot Work with Socialists," "Where We Can Work with Socialists," "The Japanese Question," and "The Thraldom of Names," a warning to readers not to fall for labels. They were the first of many.

TR stated plainly in his first editorial that the magazine would be his vehicle to support people who believed in "a wise individualism" because the magazine owners "preach the things that are most necessary to the salvation of this people." Those ideas were not necessarily a new outlook for TR, who had been espousing them for most of his life. He was off on a new adventure.

Part 8

After the Presidency

FACT #83. THE SMITHSONIAN SENT ROOSEVELT ON AN ELEVEN-MONTH SAFARI TO EAST AFRICA IN 1909.

TR was out of office with no particular plans other than writing occasional articles for *Outlook* magazine. Sitting idle was never one of his favorite pastimes. He needed something meaningful to do. The Smithsonian Institution came to the rescue and asked him to lead a scientific expedition to British East Africa, which lasted from April 21, 1909, to March 14, 1910.

The cost of the expedition was $100,000 (about $2.5 million in 2010 terms), or about $8.77 per specimen collected. (The number of specimens collected was 11,397.) The Smithsonian paid half, which it generated from requests for donations. TR added $25,000, as did Andrew Carnegie. The party included two guides, two zoologists, a physician, a photographer (TR's son Kermit), and a *bwana*, or boss.

Technically, TR was the leader, but in name only. The true leader was R.J. Cunninghame (alternately spelled Cunningham), a guide from the expedition's outfitter, Newland & Tarlton. But TR was the star of the trip. Without him, the safari might have been just one more expedition to Africa. Because it was him and he was still riding a wave of post-presidency popularity, his trip started a rash of safaris among adventurers who could afford the hefty cost.

TR was grateful for the opportunity. It gave him the chance to further his knowledge of natural history, hunt big game, and spend quality time with his son Kermit.

While in Africa, TR started coming face-to-face with his own mortality and the passing of the torch. Again, while talking about Kermit, this time in a letter to Ethel, he wrote about their last hunt together. They were successful.

Between them, they shot three giant eland. "We worked hard," TR wrote. "Kermit of course worked hardest, for he is really a first-class walker and runner; I had to go slowly, but I kept at it all day and every day." He still had the will. Some of his famed energy was lacking.

TR had always wanted to take a safari such as this one. But it provided more proof to some of his detractors that he wanted to shoot wildlife, not catalog it. He told the audience at his November 18, 1910, presentation to the National Geographic Society:

Really, I would be ashamed of myself sometimes, for I felt as if I had all the fun. I would kill the rhinoceros or whatever it was, and then [the scientists] would go out and do the solid, hard work of preparing it. They would spend a day or two preserving the specimens, while I would go and get something else.

In TR's final report to the Smithsonian, he gives the credit for the safari to the other members: "The invertebrates were collected carefully by Dr. Mearns, with some assistance from Messrs. Cunningham and Kermit Roosevelt . . . Anthropological materials were gathered by Dr. Mearns with some assistance from others; a collection was contributed by Major Ross, an American in the government service at Nairobi," etc. His report made it sound as if he did not do any of the work, which was rarely the case with TR.

Teddy Trivia

TR and Kermit combined killed 512 animals during their safari, including seventeen lions, eleven elephants, and twenty rhinoceroses. Once, while TR was standing over a freshly killed eland, a guide told him about a rhinoceros standing nearby. He rushed over and shot it, too. That was how hunters gathered "specimens" in those days.

FACT #84. ROOSEVELT COULDN'T HELP STIRRING UP CONTROVERSY WHEREVER HE WENT.

While on his European tour, TR spoke at the Guildhall in London. The Corporation of the City of London, the oldest corporation in the world, presented TR with the "Freedom of the City" on May 31, 1910. He used the occasion to present a speech on "British Rule in Africa," a subject about which he had learned a lot in his recent safari.

He began simply: "I wish to say a few words because they are true, without regard to whether or not they are pleasant."

TR was brutally direct in his choice of words. He told his audience that someone had to rule Egypt to restore order out of chaos, but they had better do it right. He advised that, "If you stay in Egypt it is your first duty to keep order, and above all things also to punish murder and to bring to justice all who directly or indirectly invite others to commit murder or condone the crime when it is committed."

Some detractors construed his meaning as an invitation to apply violence and injustice against the "fanatical" Egyptians. They also charged that he referenced the Egyptians's attempts at self-government as "farcical." "Fanatical" and "farcical" were not words he used. Regardless of his exact words, he created a worldwide firestorm.

TR's comments drew derision and criticism from people on all sides of the political spectrum, especially in London, where liberals accused him of basing his comments on a single safari to Africa rather than on any real knowledge of Egypt or Britain's role in ruling it. As TR said, truth trumped pleasantness. Per usual, truth lay in the eyes of the beholder, and the controversy he created was something to behold.

Not everything he said at Guildhall was controversial. He also said, "The people at home, whether in Europe or America, who live softly, often fail fully to realize what is being done for them by the men who are actually engaged in the pioneer work of civilization abroad." That had been true in his forays into Cuba and the Philippines. He saw it as true when he was updating the British on the status of their rule in Egypt.

He didn't just stir up the British, he also stirred up some of the people in Italy—specifically Pope Pius X.

An incident regarding a proposed visit to see Pope Pius X in Rome drew a lot of negative publicity for him. Some people labeled him anti-Catholic. The argument showed that TR could generate controversy wherever he went, even when he was just trying to enjoy himself.

TR had asked the U.S. ambassador to Italy, John G.A. Leishman Sr., to arrange an audience with the pope—if it was mutually convenient. The pope agreed to an April 5 meeting. TR wrote in a March 25 cable that if the pope did not receive him, "I shall not for a moment question the propriety of his action."

The negotiations dragged on—but never directly between the pope and TR. Eventually, the meeting fell through. Catholics believed that TR had snubbed the pope. The issue took on a larger-than-it-had-to-be life.

Critics weighed in on both sides of the issue, which became an international incident.

Gradually, the issue went away—and so did TR. He left Italy and returned to the friendlier confines of other European countries.

Teddy Trivia

Contrary to popular belief, TR did not make his Guildhall comments out of the blue. He had submitted his speech to high-ranking British government officers prior to delivering it. They had approved his remarks. He was on solid ground in what he said. Critics had never daunted him before. They did not this time, either.

FACT #85. UPON RETURNING FROM HIS POST-PRESIDENCY TOUR OF EUROPE, ROOSEVELT WAS GREETED WITH A HOMECOMING PARADE THAT ATTRACTED 1 MILLION PEOPLE.

TR did not return to the United States immediately after the African safari ended. TR allowed that he had never passed a more interesting eleven months than those he spent in Africa, especially from the standpoint of a scientist. However, it was time for a new adventure. Europe seemed like a good place to find one—especially since Edith was going to meet him there.

He traveled around Europe for a few months, giving speeches, collecting honoraria, and representing the country at King Edward VII of Great Britain's funeral.

He took a side trip to Denmark and Norway in early May to pick up his Nobel Peace Prize, since he was in the area. During his May 5 acceptance speech, the man who had urged the United States to go to war against Spain in 1898 and who would push for its entry into World War I in Europe, declared that, "Peace is generally good in itself, but it is never the highest good unless it comes as the handmaid of righteousness; and it becomes a very evil thing if it serves merely as a mask for cowardice and sloth, or as an instrument to further the ends of despotism or anarchy."

Three weeks later, he received an honorary membership in the Cambridge Union, Cambridge University's debating society. TR was in his glory during those days in Europe.

One speech in particular caught people's attention: his April 23, 1910, presentation at the Sorbonne in Paris.

In his "Citizenship in a Republic" talk, TR lauded people of action, not those who sit by idly and let others do the work:

> *It is not the critic who counts; not the man who points out how the strong man stumbles, or where the doer of deeds could have done them better. The credit belongs to the man who is actually in the arena, whose face is marred by dust*

and sweat and blood; who strives valiantly; who errs, who comes short again and again, because there is no effort without error and shortcoming; but who does actually strive to do the deeds; who knows great enthusiasms, the great devotions; who spends himself in a worthy cause; who at the best knows in the end the triumph of high achievement, and who at the worst, if he fails, at least fails while daring greatly, so that his place shall never be with those cold and timid souls who know neither victory nor defeat.

That passage caught the world's attention, and gave the listeners an insight into TR's philosophy of life.

After some months in Europe, TR returned to the United States. He arrived in New York City on June 18, 1910, aboard the ocean liner *Kaiserin Auguste Victoria.* The city staged an elaborate homecoming that attracted 1 million people. TR transferred to two revenue cutters and sailed up the Hudson River, followed by a flotilla of nearly 100 vessels of all shapes and sizes. The mayor of New York City, William J. Gaynor, and TR both gave the obligatory speeches followed by a parade up Broadway and Fifth Avenue.

Teddy Trivia

The "Welcome Home" parade for TR included nearly 2,000 veterans of the Spanish-American War. Among them were his Rough Riders, First United States Volunteer Cavalry, who preceded his open carriage. The war had been over for twelve years, but the troops' adulation for TR was still evident. And the bands played on.

FACT #86. ROOSEVELT'S ACTIONS IN THE AREA OF CONSERVATION EVENTUALLY LED TO THE FOUNDATION OF THE NATIONAL PARK SERVICE IN 1916.

TR had always been conservation-minded, but his experiences in the Badlands reinforced in his mind that need for conservation, especially in the West, where weather conditions were harsher than in the East, water was at a premium, and some animals, such as the buffalo, were being hunted to extinction for commercial purposes. Alleviating these conditions became a primary goal for TR. He began to push for conservation shortly after his return from the Badlands.

In 1887, Roosevelt and a large group of concerned conservationists founded the Boone and Crockett Club to implement their goals: to work for the elimination of industrial hunting, the creation of wildlife reserves, and a conservation-oriented regulation of hunting.

The founders of the Boone and Crockett Club included approximately twenty to twenty-five scientists, military leaders, politicians, explorers, writers, and industrialists. The group was typical of Roosevelt's alliances: eclectic and action-oriented.

TR and his conservation-minded friends, some of whom almost made saving resources a religion, had created a movement that picked up speed—and enemies. Once business leaders figured out that conservation was going to cost them money, they began to fight attempts to promote it. Even Congress fought against the conservation of natural resources at times.

Fighting with Congress and business people over the value and costs of conservation was one thing TR would not miss after he left office. Neither would he give up his own campaign to protect the nation's resources. TR redirected his efforts to private ventures, while his supporters carried on the fight in their own arenas. Together, they set a trend for future, never-ending battles over conservation issues.

TR and his conservation colleagues helped preserve more than 170 million acres of land by designating them as national parks and monuments. One of the president's last acts was to designate Mount Olympus in Washington State as a national monument—only two days before he left office in 1909.

TR's influence and efforts to push conservation lasted long after he left office. His actions in the area led to the formation of the National Park Service, which was established on August 25, 1916. That was only part of his legacy.

According to some estimates, TR placed approximately 230 million acres of natural resources under federal protection during his tenure as president. That included parks, forests, game and bird preserves, and other unique natural resources. Congress, business people, and other critics may have opposed him at times, but he succeeded in conserving huge amounts of resources for all the people of the United States.

One of TR's most enduring pieces of legislation was the Antiquities Act of 1906, which he signed on June 8 of that year. It made possible the preservation of historic, scientific, commemorative, and cultural values of the archaeological and historic sites and structures on public land. Most importantly, it obligated—and continues to obligate—the federal agencies that manage that land to act in the best interests of present and future generations.

"Present and future . . ." That highlighted TR's attitude about conversation. Not only was it intended to save natural resources for everybody of that time, but for those of future generations as well. That was typical of TR when it came to conservation—and almost everything else in which he had an interest. He was always looking ahead.

Teddy Trivia

The Boone and Crockett Club is still in existence—and still working at the same goals as when TR and his group established it. Part of its mission statement sums up TR's philosophy about hunting and conservation in general: to "support the use and enjoyment of our wildlife heritage to the fullest extent by this and future generations."

FACT #87. ROOSEVELT WASN'T JUST PRESIDENT OF THE UNITED STATES—HE WAS PRESIDENT OF THE AMERICAN HISTORICAL ASSOCIATION.

Few people in TR's circle of associates were as well versed as he was across the spectrum of academic and literary pursuits. Nevertheless, the people with whom he associated helped him develop his knowledge and skill sets even more.

More importantly, TR and his associates used their knowledge to help educate people at all levels of society. Sometimes their efforts went unrecognized. At other times, they led to controversy. In many cases, they were long-lasting. In fact, some of TR's initiatives and innovations are still affecting society today.

TR was not only a student of history, but a practicing historian as well. While he was president of the United States, he pushed for the preservation of historical records, which made him an ideal candidate for the leadership of the American Historical Association (AHA). He became the association's twenty-seventh president in 1912. One of his primary duties as president was the same as that of his predecessors and successors: give an address at the annual meeting.

TR told members in a December 27, 1912, "State of the Union" address in Boston that historians had to have imagination if they were going to be storytellers and entice the general public into developing an interest in what created their world. He declared, "The imaginative power demanded for a great historian is different from that demanded for a great poet; but it is no less marked. Such imaginative power is in no sense incompatible with minute accuracy."

As he explained, "On the contrary, very accurate, very real and vivid, presentation of the past can come only from one in whom the imaginative gift is strong."

He urged professors and historians to lighten up and become a bit more romantic in order to foster a love of history among nonprofessionals, rather than analyzing it scientifically in esoteric journals such as *The American Historical Review*, which few people other than themselves read or understood. There was a certain irony in his suggestion. TR was less than enthralled with the "nature fakers" who used that romantic approach in their natural history storytelling. Nevertheless, he averred that historians apply a bit of it in their writing.

In TR's opinion, historians' purposes were to be great moralists and to "thrill the souls of men with stories of strength and craft and daring." He said that he hoped when the history of his era was written, "It will show the forces working for good in our national life outweigh [those] working for evil." That summed up his personal philosophy about government and history. TR worked for good throughout his lifetime, in every capacity in which he served.

Fact #88. Roosevelt coined the term "nature fakers."

A controversy arose in the United States in the early 1900s over whether animals were governed by instinct, instruction, or intuition and how they should be presented in literature.

Readers enjoyed stories like Anna Sewell's *Black Beauty* (1890); Jack London's *White Fang* (a sequel to his 1903 bestseller, *The Call of the Wild*, which appeared in serial form in *Outing* magazine prior to its publication in book form in 1906); and William Long's *Brier-Patch Philosophy* (appearing in *Harper's Monthly* starting in early 1905 under the pseudonym Peter Rabbit). As innocuous as such stories were, they generated significant literary controversy.

Stories of the generic genre irritated true naturalists such as John Burroughs and William Morton Wheeler, who abhorred the fact that writers untrained in animal science were leading people to believe erroneously that some critters had human tendencies. Worse, as Burroughs and his supporters suggested, these pseudo-naturalists were writing more to earn money than to educate readers about what really drove animals to do what they did, namely instinct.

Though he stayed out of the debate at first, TR believed that animals existed solely to satisfy human needs, especially in the name of progress, so it didn't matter what prompted them to act. Eventually, he had enough of the debate and jumped into it, ostensibly to protect his friend John Burroughs.

Ever since TR had acquired the seal's skull and shot his first buffalo, he had retained his fascination with natural history. In fact—and identifying facts as opposed to fiction was the gist of the "Nature Fakers" controversy—it was their mutual interest in natural history that began TR's friendship with Burroughs, which started when they explored Yellowstone Park together in 1903. It was only natural that Roosevelt would try to defend him.

The catalyst that finally drew TR into the debate was a book by writer, naturalist, and Congregational minister William Joseph Long, titled *Northern Trails*. In it, Long described how one of his subjects, a wolf named Wayeeses, killed a caribou by impaling its heart with his teeth.

As a hunter, TR knew that it was a physical impossibility for a wolf to do that. So the president wrote a letter to the publisher with a copy to Burroughs in which he pointed out that Long's description was inane. TR's personal involvement in the "Nature Fakers" controversy had begun. He became a crusader against nature fiction writers such as Long, Jack London, the Canadian poet Charles G.D. Roberts, and Ernest Thompson Seton. He charged them with writing "unnatural history."

London labeled TR in a *Collier's* magazine article as "homocentric" and "amateur." Long suggested that the president had no room to talk when it came to understanding nature. He wrote, "I find after carefully reading two of his big books that every time he gets near the heart of a wild thing he invariably puts a bullet through it."

Eventually, TR withdrew from the debate and returned to his presidential duties.

About the only significant outcome of the debate was TR's contribution to the lexicon of the day; he coined the term "nature fakers." He took the name from an article in the June 1907 issue of *Everybody's Magazine* by journalist Edward B. Clark, which was based on his interview with the president.

Clark entitled the article "Roosevelt on the Nature Fakirs." TR changed the spelling of fakirs in an essay he wrote, in which he charged that "nature fakers" completely "deceive many good people who are wholly ignorant of wild life." The term caught on, and TR got the credit for it.

FACT #89. ROOSEVELT INSPIRED THE NAME FOR THE "TEDDY BEAR."

After his first wife Alice died, TR wanted people to stop calling him "Teddy," which was her nickname for him. In this, he was not successful. Now he is forever connected with the "teddy bear," which his name popularized. Inadvertently, the "teddy bear" became one of the world's most beloved toys.

In November 1902, TR went on a bear hunt to Mississippi, but game was difficult to find. Eventually, the hunting dogs cornered a small black bear (in some versions of the story, his hunting partners found and captured a bear for him to shoot, since they felt sorry for the avid hunter having such bad luck). Party members asked TR to kill the bear, but he felt it was unsporting and refused.

The Boone and Crockett Club, a conservationist and hunting organization that TR had helped to found, had (and still has) a code of ethics requiring hunters to follow the rules of "fair chase," which they define as "the ethical, sportsmanlike, and lawful pursuit and taking of any free-ranging wild, native North American big game animal in a manner that does not give the hunter an improper advantage over such animals." TR, the man who coined the phrase "square deal," of course had to follow the code.

Based on this story, artist Clifford K. Berryman of the *Washington Post* created an amusing cartoon called "Drawing the line in Mississippi."

The cartoon delighted readers and prompted several toy makers to manufacture stuffed toy bears named for the president.

Allegedly one of the toy manufacturers wrote to Roosevelt to get his permission, which Roosevelt granted.

A series of children's books by Seymour Eaton, called The Roosevelt Bears, followed the adventures of a pair of anthropomorphic bears named after the president (Teddy-B and Teddy-G). These children's books were popular for many years.

FACT #90. ROOSEVELT WAS THE FIRST SITTING OR FORMER PRESIDENT TO RIDE IN AN AIRPLANE (IN 1910).

On October 11, 1910, TR became the first sitting or former U.S. president to fly in an airplane when he took a flight with Arch Hoxsey in St. Louis, Missouri. He was attending the Missouri State Republican Party's convention when Hoxsey invited him to take a ride in his biplane. TR took him up on the offer, somewhat reluctantly.

In keeping with his flamboyant character, TR arrived at the Kinloch aviation field in a motorcade replete with local dignitaries. They included the governor of Missouri, Herbert S. Hadley, the mayor of St. Louis, Henry W. Kiel, and Sheriff Louis Nolte. He watched as Hoxsey inspected the plane. Then they climbed aboard and took off.

Hoxsey had just completed a record flight of 104 miles from Springfield, Illinois, to St. Louis. His flight with TR took considerably less time.

Hoxsey got the plane as high as fifty feet off the ground, circled the field twice, and stayed in the air for only four minutes. TR said later that he wished he could have flown for an hour.

Once the short flight ended, TR stepped off the plane, mingled with the crowd, got into his automobile, and drove away. It was an anticlimactic moment for him and another presidential (or past-presidential) first.

TR had another connection with planes: His son became a pilot during World War I. Quentin was at Harvard when WWI began. He dropped out to join the army and train as a pilot. Two German aviators shot him down behind their lines in France on July 14, 1918—Bastille Day.

At first, the Germans did not know who he was. As far as they knew, he was just another American pilot who had died fighting for freedom. They learned quickly that was not the case. Allegedly, Germans found a letter on Quentin's body from his fiancée, Flora Payne Whitney. That is how they identified him. She had wanted to travel to Europe to marry Quentin while he was stationed there. Permission was denied.

Once the Germans discovered that the deceased pilot was TR's son, they buried him with honors where he had fallen. Approximately 1,000 Germans formed an honor guard near the crash site. They marked his grave with a wooden cross and the wheels and propellers from his plane.

The cross carried these simple words: "Lieutenant Roosevelt, buried by the Germans."

Teddy Trivia

Taking TR for a short flight got Hoxsey in trouble with the Wright brothers. Hoxsey, who had been trained by Orville Wright, was flying as part of their exhibition team. The Wrights almost fired him because they thought flying celebrities such as TR was too dangerous. They did not want to be responsible if anything went wrong.

FACT #91. ROOSEVELT, DISILLUSIONED WITH PRESIDENT TAFT'S POLICIES, CREATED A NEW POLITICAL PARTY TO CHALLENGE HIM FOR THE PRESIDENCY IN 1912.

When Taft assumed office in 1909, TR was sure he would follow a progressive agenda. By mid-1910 it was clear that he would not. Worse than not following the agenda, he appeared to be trying to rid the Republican Party of its progressive wing. That was anathema to TR's thinking.

During the 1910 Republican Party primaries, Taft took steps to eliminate progressives from the party. He was afraid that they would challenge his programs and policies if they were elected. For the most part—and uncharacteristically—TR stayed out of the political maneuvering. All Taft succeeded in doing was splitting the party and alienating voters.

The year 1911 was a rare one for TR. He did not publish any books, and the number of speeches he gave dwindled. That gave him more time to follow politics and fret about President Taft's swing away from TR's idea of what he should be doing. That did not bode well for Taft or the Republican Party.

The schism between Taft and the progressives in the Republican Party developed over several key issues, primarily conservation, tariff reform, and foreign policy. TR took some of Taft's changes personally, which could only mean a confrontation between his and the president's supporters. TR may have been out of office, but he preferred to see his policies remain intact.

TR decided to run for president again in 1912. He and Taft had gone their separate ways, and TR saw a need to get the United States back on track. He believed he was the right man to correct what he perceived as needing correction. TR went from private citizen to presidential candidate once again.

The differences between the progressive and conservative factions of the Republican Party regarding tariffs, conservation, foreign affairs, and other policies created a schism. The door was open for a challenger to Taft for the presidency in the 1912 election or a third-party candidate.

Once TR made it known that he was willing to run for president, supporters flocked to his side.

Even though TR had a commanding lead in the delegate count, the numbers were misleading. The national party leaders actually had the last say in whose delegates got seated at the convention. Taft still had a lot of support within the party. As a result, there were 254 delegate seats contested prior to the convention. The Republican National Committee awarded 235 of them to Taft and 19 to TR. The campaign that had looked so promising went up in smoke.

When it became evident that Taft was going to win the nomination, TR and the bulk of his delegates walked away from the convention. They formed their own party and urged TR to head it. He agreed. So was born the "Bull Moose" Party.

The defectors named their new faction the Progressive Party, met in Chicago for their own convention in August 1912, and named TR as their presidential candidate, with Governor Hiram W. Johnson of California, a cofounder of the Progressive Party, as his vice president. When someone asked TR if he was healthy enough to run for president, he retorted that he was "fit as a bull moose." TR put his stamp on the new party, which became known from that point on as the "Bull Moose" Party.

Fact #92. Roosevelt was the first national politician to include women in party politics.

TR's supporters rallied to his side as his presidential campaign began. He had a penchant for affiliating with people who would be helpful to him when their support was needed. The presidential race of 1912 was one of those times. Some surprising people allied with him, and he found a new cause or two to espouse.

On the other hand, some surprising people turned away from TR. Among them was his son-in-law, Nicholas Longworth. TR's daughter Alice sided with her father. That strained the Longworth's marriage, which had never been that strong to begin with. TR was grateful for his daughter's support.

One of the surprising elements of the 1912 presidential campaign was the role women played in it. TR had always been supportive of women and children, starting with his sisters and continuing through his political career. Therefore, it should not have surprised anyone that women received a voice in the Bull Moose Party's campaign.

There were several women in attendance at the Bull Moose convention in Chicago. They included doctors, lawyers, college professors, social workers, and other professionals. The women played a large role.

Prior to 1912, women had not played a significant role in national politics. If TR had not included them in the Bull Moose Party's campaign in 1912, that trend would have continued. Neither President Taft nor the Democratic candidate, Woodrow Wilson, supported women's suffrage nationally. Only women in a few Western states even had the right to vote, let alone participate in political campaigns. TR changed that.

Jane Addams seconded TR's nomination for president. That was the first time a female had ever spoken at a large political party's national convention.

In another step toward progress, the Bull Moose Party mandated four women as members-at-large on the Progressive National Committee. That was another first in the fight for women's suffrage. It ensured that females would be represented at the top of the party's leadership structure. That was a politically popular move among the progressives and drew some significant support for TR.

The participation of women in the Progressive Party movement gave them a new voice in American politics, and thrust some females into national prominence. Ostensibly, TR's focus on women's suffrage helped him carry California and Washington. At least one woman, Helen Scott, of Washington, cast a vote for him in the Electoral College that year.

Historians debate whether Helen Scott was actually the first woman in U.S. history to cast an Electoral College vote. It is possible, but unsubstantiated, that some women in California were Progressive Party electors in the 1912 presidential election. Either way, females did cast Electoral College votes in 1912, which was a major step forward for women's suffrage—thanks to TR.

Teddy Trivia

Jane Addams was an innovative social reformer who attempted to bring people at different economic, ethnic, and social levels closer together in interdependent communities that featured settlement houses. The best known was Hull House, founded in Chicago in 1889 by Jane Addams and Ellen Gates Starr. Addams was also the first woman to win the Nobel Peace Prize, in 1931.

Fact #93. On October 14, 1912, an attempt to assassinate Roosevelt was made.

Though he knew he was a long shot to win the presidential race as a third-party candidate, TR campaigned tirelessly. He scheduled a speech in Milwaukee three weeks before the election.

On the night of his Milwaukee speech, TR left his hotel at about 8 P.M. to head via automobile for the Milwaukee Auditorium, the site of his scheduled oration. TR stood on the floorboard of the vehicle, waving to the crowd, as he headed for the auditorium.

Events moved fast and in a confused fashion. John Schrank, who was merely carrying out his duty as he told the police later, raised his pistol and aimed it at TR. A bystander, Adam Bittner, saw what was happening. He hit Schrank's arm as the gun went off. The deflected bullet tore into TR. The bullet Schrank fired almost point-blank hit TR's steel eyeglass case, traveled through the fifty-page manuscript of his speech, and entered his chest near the right nipple.

Members of the crowd started pummeling Schrank rather brutally, and there were cries to hang him on the spot. Some people even headed for nearby stores to find ropes. TR came to Schrank's rescue. "Don't hurt the poor creature," he implored the crowd. Some of them were stunned that TR was able to talk, let alone stand and speak. But, they acceded to his wishes and let the man alone.

TR did not have much of a comment after the incident. He did say later, "I did not care a rap for being shot." He added that, "It is a trade risk, which every prominent public man ought to accept as a matter of course."

TR completed his journey to the auditorium and delivered his scheduled speech to the 10,000 people assembled there. They knew nothing about the assassination attempt.

He mentioned it to them with a terse statement:

Friends, I shall ask you to be as quiet as possible. I don't know whether you fully understand that I have just been shot; but it takes more than that to kill a Bull Moose. But fortunately I had my manuscript, so you see I was going to make a long speech, and there is a bullet—there is where the bullet went through—and it probably saved me from it going into my heart. The bullet is in me now, so that I cannot make a very long speech, but I will try my best.

Then he spoke for ninety minutes!

TR's Milwaukee speech effectively ended his campaign. He was admitted to a hospital for treatment, where he stayed for a week. Doctors opted not to remove it, since surgery was risky and could cause more damage than the actual shot. It was still in his chest when he died a little over six years later.

Out of respect, Taft and Wilson stopped campaigning, too. They resumed when TR was released from the hospital. TR did not. Except for one appearance at Madison Square Garden in New York City on October 30, all he could do was sit back and await the election results, which were disappointing.

Teddy Trivia

The Bavarian-born John Schrank was an itinerant ex–tavern keeper from New York City. He allegedly shot TR to deliver a message to U.S. presidents that they should not serve three terms. Schrank was never tried for shooting TR. Doctors pronounced him insane. Schrank was held for thirty years in mental hospitals in Wisconsin until he died in 1943.

FACT #94. ROOSEVELT WAS THE ONLY THIRD-PARTY CANDIDATE TO EVER PLACE SECOND IN A PRESIDENTIAL ELECTION.

TR had established a lot of firsts in his career. He set another one in the 1912 presidential election, but it was not a particularly satisfying first for him. Woodrow Wilson won the election, but TR finished second. As a result, he became the first—and only—third-party candidate in U.S. political history to place second in a presidential election.

It was a dubious distinction, but TR was also the first major third-party candidate to become the victim of an assassination attempt. John Schrank told police after he shot TR, "Any man looking for a third term ought to be shot." At first, that was all he had to say, and he repeated his statement several times before he gave a full confession.

Wilson won the 1912 presidential election in a landslide. He earned 6,296,284 votes (41.84 percent), compared to TR's 4,122,721 (27.4 percent) and Taft's 3,486,242 (23.2 percent). In the all-important Electoral College voting, Wilson won 435 votes; TR had eighty-eight. The incumbent, Taft, received the remaining eight. The TR-Taft split gave Wilson the victory. For TR, second place just was not good enough.

The Roosevelt-Johnson ticket won only six states: Washington, California, South Dakota, Minnesota, Michigan, and Pennsylvania. They won California by the narrowest of margins—174 votes. TR had 283,610 to Wilson's 283,436. That was due to Johnson's popularity in the state and possibly the ticket's support for women's suffrage, not necessarily because Californians liked TR.

And Wisconsin? Wilson collected 164,230 votes, Taft got 130,596, and TR gathered a paltry 62,448. The people of the state where he had literally been shot figuratively shot him down.

Numbers of votes aside, TR had done quite well for a third-party candidate.

Once the 1912 presidential election ended, TR's version of the Progressive Party disappeared. Progressivism itself did not. TR returned to the Republican Party, but his foray into "Bull Moose" territory was not in vain. Once again, he initiated responses in the political life of the United States with his call for a "New Nationalism."

Significant outcomes of the Bull Moose Party included a new push for federal regulation in a variety of areas. Another was the birth of the primary system. TR and his progressive cronies had demonstrated that presidential hopefuls who did not adhere to the platforms of the two major parties had access to a new system of choosing candidates—or at least the opportunity to have their voices heard.

The Bull Moose Party went out of business almost as quickly as it had entered the American political scene. It lasted for only four years, but its short life was not in vain. Thanks to TR and his charismatic leadership, the party left a legacy that progressives could build on. Once again he had influenced the country, even in defeat.

TR lost an election but gained more respect from his fellow Americans—at least some of them. But, as far as presidential elections go, second- or third-place finishes are meaningless to the runners-up.

Neither one is first. TR was still out of a job after the 1912 presidential election ended.

FACT #95. AFTER LOSING THE ELECTION, ROOSEVELT EMBARKED ON AN EIGHT-MONTH EXPEDITION TO SOUTH AMERICA.

TR had put a lot of effort into the presidential campaign of 1912, and it had taken a lot out of him. But, opportunity always knew where to find TR. It found its way to his door once again via his friend, Father John Augustine Zahm, a University of Notre Dame–educated Roman Catholic priest.

TR's son Kermit was living and working in South America at the time, and the chance to explore with him once again intrigued TR. He accepted the invitation—and contributed $5,000 to help underwrite the venture.

As things turned out, the trip became more than he had bargained for. The expedition lasted for eight months, from October 4, 1913, to May 19, 1914—and may have contributed to shortening TR's life.

What began as a speaking tour for TR morphed into an exploration of the Rio da Dúvida (River of Doubt) in the Amazon region of Brazil, so named by an explorer who discovered its headwaters but had no idea of where it flowed—and no desire to find out. The expedition included Father Zahm, naturalists George K. Cherrie and Leo E. Miller, Kermit Roosevelt, Cândido Rondon, and porters and helpers. (Miller was the nominal leader of the expedition.)

The trip was harrowing for TR and his companions. The events would have been the basis for a good adventure movie.

The explorers spent six weeks traveling down the River of Doubt, encountering a never-ending series of rapids and waterfalls. They lost five of their seven canoes and three members of the expedition during the trip (four, counting a dog) and had to build new canoes. One member drowned accidentally in rapids. His body was never recovered. Two others were murdered by a porter.

During one stretch of forty-eight days they did not see another human being. That was probably a good thing, since the area was populated by tribes of violent natives who were not above killing strangers in their land.

TR contracted malaria during the expedition, the old "Cuban fever" that had affected him in 1898. To make matters worse, he had cut his leg during the trip. The wound had not healed properly, and the infection led to severe bleeding, swelling, and a temperature of 105 degrees. The combination of malaria and infection drove TR to despair—and to thoughts of suicide. He was at such a low point that he told the party to go on without him.

At the height of his illness, the expedition stopped at a series of waterfalls that seemed impassable to the leaders. TR was of no value to them. He was laid up in the expedition's one remaining tent. The situation was dire, to say the least.

Eventually, Kermit devised a way to lower the party's boats over some waterfalls and saved the surviving members of the expedition. As a result, they succeeded finally in mapping a previously uncharted river, which the Brazilian government renamed after TR. He and his colleagues had paid a heavy price for the honor.

Even though TR did not pay for the trip with his life immediately, the illnesses and injuries he incurred certainly played a role in his deteriorating health over the next few years.

Teddy Trivia

TR laid out the details of the exploration trip in a May 1, 1914, letter to the Brazilian minister of foreign affairs, Lauro Müller. He closed the letter with, "My dear Sir, I thank you from my heart for the chance to take part in this great work of exploration." With his typical humility, not once did he mention the injuries, illness, or resulting severe depression that afflicted him during the expedition.

FACT #96. ROOSEVELT CRITICIZED PRESIDENT WILSON AND CAMPAIGNED AGAINST HIM.

After TR returned from South America, he began filling pages of various publications with articles and editorials on a wide range of topics. Initially, they were narratives of his expedition, some of which he had been writing while traveling. As 1914 wore on, his focus changed to politics, particularly criticizing the president and his policies.

Among the articles TR published in late 1914 were "Women and the New York Constitutional Convention" (*Outlook*, August 1), "The Right of the People to Review Judge-Made Law" (*Outlook*, August 8), "The Danger of Making Unwise Peace Treaties" (*New York Times*, October 10), and "The Navy as a Peacemaker" (*New York Times*, November 22). He was making his views of Wilson's policies public.

TR was not attacking President Wilson personally, even though he disagreed with him on almost everything. Personal attacks would come later, especially in the presidential election campaign of 1916. In true political fashion, he disguised his messages nicely as he presented opposing views.

TR was especially critical of what he considered Wilson's timid response to American involvement in World War I, which began in the summer of 1914. At first, the president encouraged Americans to stay out of it, even in the face of attacks on American ships and citizens, such as the sinking of the *Lusitania*.

The Bull Moose Party encouraged TR to head its ticket in the 1916 presidential election. But he declined. He had learned a lesson from his third-party experience in 1912 and recognized that his chances of winning under the Bull Moose banner were small. He wanted the Republican Party nomination.

He didn't get it. The Republicans nominated Charles E. Hughes on the third ballot. TR met with Hughes after his nomination, then withdrew from the race and threw his support to Hughes and campaigned actively on his behalf. His speeches tended to be bombastic and prowar. Whether that helped Hughes is a matter of speculation. TR did launch direct criticisms against President Wilson, which did not help Hughes's candidacy in some quarters.

TR suggested that the Wilson administration had neglected the navy to the point that it had affected "the efficiency of the fleet and the enthusiasm of its officers and men." Two days earlier, in Denver, in his oration, "Preparedness: Military, Industrial and Spiritual," he attributed the country's lack of preparation for war to "evil leadership given our people in high places." He opined that "Mr. Wilson has not only been too proud to fight, but has also been too proud to prepare."

In one of his last campaign speeches, on November 4, in Bridgeport, Connecticut, he went all out. He criticized Wilson's foreign policy, rallied for United States intervention in Mexico's internal political upheavals, and attacked hyphenated citizenship such as Irish-American, Italian-American, etc. TR said there was "no room in this country for those whose loyalty was 'fifty-fifty.'"

He even took a swipe at Secretary of War Newton D. Baker, who he labeled "a noble gentleman who, I understand, knits well." That was an apparent slap at Wilson's reluctance to enter the war. The Bridgeport audience did not take too kindly to TR's comments. There was some heckling, but it was not the first time political opponents had chided TR.

If nothing else, TR's fiery speeches were attracting attention. But, they may not have been conducive to winning support for Hughes. President Wilson won the election.

FACT #97. ROOSEVELT'S REQUEST TO LEAD A REGIMENT IN WORLD WAR I WAS DENIED.

After Wilson won re-election, TR went back to his private life; the United States entered the war—and TR had the audacity to petition the president to rejoin the army.

President Wilson found that he had no choice but to involve the United States in World War I. German submarines were sinking American merchant ships at an alarming rate, and Germany had invited Mexico to join it in the war against the United States.

German Foreign Minister Zimmermann sent the German minister in Mexico an enciphered message on January 16, 1917, that proposed a German-Mexican alliance. Germany offered to Mexico the return of the territory it lost in the Mexican-American War. However, British intelligence intercepted, deciphered, and forwarded the message to American authorities on February 24. Its contents raised some eyebrows in the United States.

Finally, Congress declared war on Germany, only a month after the president—who ran on the slogan that he kept the country out of it—began his second term. Two months earlier TR had requested permission from the president to raise, equip, and lead a division of volunteers for service in France.

TR fully expected that he would become involved in World War I. In a May 18, 1917, letter to President Wilson, he wrote:

I respectfully ask permission immediately to raise two divisions for immediate service at the front under the bill which has just become law, and hold myself ready to raise four divisions, if you so direct. I respectfully refer for details to my last letters to the Secretary of War [Newton D. Baker].

With his usual optimism, TR believed his request would be granted. He already had his officers picked out. However, there were too many factors working against him to get Wilson to go along with his request.

TR was fifty-nine years old, a bit old for military duty. He was in poor health, and he already had one bullet in him. TR had insulted President Wilson both during the 1916 presidential campaign—and before it. The odds were that his request would be denied. It was.

President Wilson did not waste any time making a decision. He sent TR a terse note two days later, stating:

I very much regret that I cannot comply with the request in your telegram of yesterday. The reasons I have stated in a public statement made this morning, and I need not assure you that my conclusions were based entirely upon imperative considerations of public policy and not upon personal or private choice.

It had been a gallant, heroic, and perhaps quixotic effort on TR's part, but he would have to fight the war vicariously through his sons, all of whom volunteered for military service.

There was nothing else for TR to do. Ever the good soldier, he notified his supporters that he would not be going to war, saying, "As good

American citizens we loyally obey the decision of the Commander-in-Chief of the American Army and Navy." He returned to heckling the president and planning a possible presidential run in 1920. TR would not live long enough to carry out his plan.

Fact #98. All of Roosevelt's sons fought in World War I.

TR and Edith raised their children to be patriotic and philanthropic. That lesson never shone through more than when World War I began. The family did its part during the war—and paid a huge price.

There was no doubt that the Roosevelts would do their part. Shortly after a German U-boat sank the *Lusitania*, Theodore Jr. wrote to his brother Kermit, "I believe war is thoroughly possible . . . Should war be declared of course we all will go." Their part in the war was preordained.

There was no doubt that TR had earned the world's respect by the time World War I started. It was a war he believed had to be fought, and he made no secret of that. He had encouraged President Wilson to get the country involved and had even offered to raise a regiment and lead it into battle. Wilson declined, and TR had to participate vicariously through his sons' military exploits.

All four of TR's sons fought in Europe. Archie, an army infantry officer, was wounded in March 1918. Kermit served with the British Expeditionary Force. Theodore Jr., also an army infantry officer, was gassed once and wounded on July 18, 1918. All three also served in World War II. Quentin was killed in action on July 14, 1918.

Almost everyone pitched in. Ethel, who was married to Dr. Richard Derby, served overseas as a Red Cross nurse at the American Ambulance Hospital in Paris, where her husband was a surgeon. Later, he served with the U.S. Army Medical Corps. He caught pneumonia in 1918 while in the army.

Theodore Jr.'s wife, Eleanor Alexander-Roosevelt, volunteered with the YMCA and worked in Paris. TR had a lot to be proud of, even if he could not serve on the frontlines himself. But Quentin's death meant heartbreak for Edith and TR.

Inwardly, TR and Edith accepted Quentin's death with a great deal of sadness. Outwardly, they put on a brave front for the world. He issued a simple statement saying, "Quentin's mother and I are very glad that he got to the front and had a chance to render some service to his country and show the stuff that was in him before his fate befell him." He had done the same himself twenty years earlier.

Ten days after Quentin died, TR wrote two letters, one to French statesman and scholar Gabriel Hanotaux, the other to his son Archie. He said essentially the same thing to both men. To Hanotaux he wrote, "It is very hard for the old to stay . . . whereas the young die in their glorious golden morning. It is bitter for me to sit at home in ease and comfort and have my four sons and my son-in-law and all the young kinsmen I have at the front facing death and enduring hardship."

He said to Archie, "It is very dreadful; it is the old who ought to die, and not fine and gallant youth with the golden morning of life still ahead; but after all he died as the heroes of old died." But, he concluded with the same convictions he had about the family's participation in World War I, "If our country did not contain such men it would not be our country."

The fact that the Germans, although they were fighting the Americans at the time, buried Quentin with honors was a grand measure of respect for TR. He did not have long to appreciate it. TR died six months later, leaving behind a legacy filled with respect.

Teddy Trivia

The American Ambulance Field Service was made up of a small group of noncombatant ambulance drivers and medical specialists who volunteered for duty in France in WWI. Inspector General of the Field Service A. Piatt Andrew said of them, they "can best be thought of as only a symbol of millions of other Americans, men and women, who would gladly have welcomed an opportunity to do what these men have done—or more."

FACT #99. ROOSEVELT WAS PREPARING TO RUN FOR PRESIDENT AGAIN IN 1920.

In a way, President Wilson might have been better off accepting TR's offer to go to France. There, TR would have been out of the president's hair for a while. Instead, TR contented himself with attacking the president's policies and setting himself up for a possible presidential run in 1920.

TR became more outspoken against Wilson's policies as the war dragged on. He used his continuing personal popularity to promote the united Republican Party principles in an effort to sway the congressional elections of 1918 back into the party's power. (The Progressive Party had all but disappeared by 1918.) He succeeded.

The Republicans gained twenty-five seats in the 1918 House of Representatives election. The Democrats lost twenty-two. That gave the Republicans a 240–192 majority in the House. (There were also one Prohibition Party member, one Farmer-Labor Party member, and one Socialist, whom the House refused to seat.) The Republican majority put added pressure on President Wilson as he sought a suitable peace treaty.

The outcome of the election not only gave the Republicans more leverage in domestic and foreign policies, but it re-established TR as a viable presidential candidate in the upcoming 1920 election.

TR was sounding like a candidate in 1918. An article in the October issue of *Metropolitan* magazine, "The Men Who Pay with Their Bodies for Their Souls' Desire," resembled a campaign platform. Although it sounded like a paean to the troops returning from the war, it laid out a plan for everything from education to unemployment insurance.

In the article, TR called for the implementation of many ideas he had been proposing for years. "The teaching in the schools should be only in English; in this country there is room for but one flag and but for one language," he averred. He suggested that there should be universal military service and "training and service in the duties of peace"—for men and women.

Other recommendations included preparing shipping for times of peace, dealing on a national scale with factory and industrial conditions, and providing old age, health, and unemployment insurance for workers. He was outlining a wide political agenda.

At all times TR was particularly critical of President Wilson's proposal for a League of Nations, which he had offered after the war ended. He wrote in a January 1919 *Metropolitan* magazine article, "If the League of Nations is built on a document as high-sounding and as meaningless as a speech in which Mr. Wilson laid down his fourteen points, it will simply add one more scrap to the diplomatic waste paper basket."

The speech to which TR referred was delivered by President Wilson to Congress in January 1918. In it, he outlined the fourteen points that formed the basis for a peace program and the November 1918 armistice between Germany and the allied countries. Point fourteen read, "A League of Nations should be set up to guarantee the political and territorial independence of all states."

The armistice might have served as an issue of contention for TR in the 1920 presidential election. Sadly, he did not get to use it.

Fact #100. Roosevelt died on January 6, 1919, after writing an editorial for *Metropolitan* magazine.

The March 19, 1919, issue of *Metropolitan* magazine carried an article by TR, titled "Bring the Fighting Men Home." The editor added a note to it:

On January 2 Colonel Roosevelt dictated this article to his secretary, Miss Strickler, who took it to him on Saturday, January 4. One of the last things he did on the Sunday evening before his death was to correct the typewritten copy.

There was one final irony in TR's death. His last editorial reflected the deeply religious old political and military warrior's final act. The God he so deeply respected did indeed bring the fighting man home.

Theodore Roosevelt died at his home in Sagamore Hill, New York, on January 6, 1919, of a pulmonary embolism. The world had lost a great leader—but it retained fond memories of a lasting legacy.

In the end, TR suffered the fate of all mortals and received the same sendoff: a funeral. And, like so many other funerals, it was a dignified, simple affair. Even though TR led a full public life, he had managed to keep much of what really mattered to him private. So it was with his funeral.

Two days after he died, 500 invited guests assembled in Christ Church (Episcopal) at Oyster Bay for a 1 P.M. celebration of his life. Another 3,000–4,000 people stood outside. The number of mourners was limited by the size of the church.

Given the opportunity, countless more would have been in attendance to say goodbye to their hero, the man known affectionately as the "American Lion." Even in death, his name lived on, as did his list of "firsts."

The funeral ceremony was simple. There was no music and no one delivered a eulogy. Even prayers were limited. Church rector Father George E. Talmage read TR's favorite hymn, "How Firm a Foundation," and said a prayer written by Cardinal John Henry Newman, which was allegedly Quentin's favorite. It was a simple sendoff for a complex man.

Following the conclusion of the ceremony, TR's coffin was placed in the hearse and carried slowly to the top of a hill at Youngs Memorial Cemetery. There, he lies in solitary repose looking out on the sea he loved—and the world he did so much to bring together.

After his funeral, the British held memorial services at Westminster Abbey in London, marking the first time a non-British person received that honor.

The fortunate 500 mourners in the church at Oyster Bay and the thousands of people who stood outside might have buried their friend that day, but they could not—and did not—bury their memories of him. They remain, in the form of TR's legacy, which may never be buried.

Teddy Trivia

Pallbearers led by TR's son Archibald carried him into the church. He rested in an oak coffin covered with the American flag, two Rough Rider regimental banners, and a wreath of laurel and yellow acacia sent by the Rough Riders. The yellow, the color of the cavalry, symbolized one of TR's most cherished memories—and the enduring love of the men he led in war.

FACT #101. ROOSEVELT'S LEGACY IS CARVED IN STONE. LITERALLY.

As long as Mount Rushmore and old movies exist, so will the memories of Theodore Roosevelt. Memories, in the form of a legacy, are the true gauge of how significant an impact a person has had on the world he has left behind. Few people in history have left as large a footprint as did Theodore Roosevelt.

One of the most recognizable reminders of TR is his profile carved on Mount Rushmore, in Keystone, South Dakota. His face is there alongside Thomas Jefferson's, George Washington's, and Abraham Lincoln's. Every time Mount Rushmore appears in a television ad or his image or persona is featured in movies, such as the *Night at the Museum* films, people are reminded of TR.

But sculptures on mountainsides and portrayals in movies do not tell the real story of historical figures. That is especially true where the legacy of Theodore Roosevelt is concerned.

One movie that prominently featured Mount Rushmore was *North by Northwest*, starring Cary Grant as Roger Thornhill. During a chase around the profiles, Thornhill said, "I don't like the way Teddy Roosevelt is looking at me." That may have been a throwaway line in a movie, but it explains in part why TR is so well remembered. He made a lot of people uncomfortable over his lifetime as he built his legacy—but pleased many more.

TR is remembered for his determined campaigns to eliminate greed and corruption in his political positions, such as New York state assemblyman, New York state governor, New York City police commissioner, and president of the United States. He fought for social justice and righteousness incessantly, in and out of office—and he did it all from a standpoint of character and righteousness.

"Character" and "righteousness" epitomize TR's life; they steered every action he undertook. Those traits may not have seemed evident to everybody with whom he was involved, but they were the basis of his personal ethos.

One of TR's most significant legacies was the impact he had on the office of U.S. president. He altered the U.S. political system by drawing attention to the role of the president in the government structure and making character as important as the issues. That was due in part to his personality—and changing technology.

TR recognized that the "bully pulpit" he had inherited as the result of President McKinley's assassination provided him with an opportunity to influence the people of the United States and the role the country played in the world. He applied his "big stick" philosophy across the globe and let the world know the United States was going to flex its muscles whenever it was required to do so.

Teddy Trivia

TR wrote to John Hay in 1897, "Is America a weakling, to shrink from the work of the great world powers? No! The young giant of the West stands on a continent and clasps the crest of an ocean in either hand. Our nation, glorious in youth and strength, looks into the future with eager eyes and rejoices as a strong man to run a race."

Index